The Golden Path to Retirement

Transform your Mindset of Retirement, Overcome Procrastination, & Take Early Action to Achieve Lifelong Wealth With Clarity & Confidence

Troy Brexton

A Quick Gift for Readers

Before You Begin

Thank you for picking up this book—I'm truly glad you're here.

If you'd like to go deeper, I regularly share **bonus chapters, exclusive content, and early previews** through my BookFunnel VIP list. It's a simple way to get even more value from what you've already started here.

Claim your free bonus here:

https://dl.bookfunnel.com/z7tc76rqrj

Let's keep learning, growing, and thriving—together.

Contents

Introduction

Have you considered what your life might look like in retirement if you stay on your current trajectory? Many believe they are set for life after years of hard work, yet the reality often paints a different picture. I have seen firsthand that a significant portion of the population is unprepared for retirement.

What's worse, many people aren't even interested in planning for retirement at all. They don't think and worry about their life in the next 10, 20, and 50 years from now because it seems so far away. When this is your mentality, it's easy to unconsciously think everything will be alright. However, this lack of readiness can lead to an uncertain future, where many might have to keep working for money due to the lack of income source, making their dream of luxurious retirement a fantasy.

I have personally seen this in my clients. No matter how much money you make, you can choose to prepare for your future or completely squander it away with lavish vacations, a fanciful lifestyle, or even just small transactions that build over time. The actions you make today could either benefit or harm your future self. Whether you are in your 20s or approaching your 60s, the time to act is now. Time keeps going forward, no matter what circumstance you are in. It doesn't even care whether you are on the right path or not. Every moment spent without proper planning is a moment that could have been invested toward securing a stable future.

I wrote this book to encourage you to think and plan for retirement proactively and strategically. Early preparation offers numerous benefits, including financial security, peace of mind, and the ability to enjoy life on your terms. By shifting focus from saving to investing, you can see the true potential of your earnings.

In this book, we will discuss the transition from being a saver to becoming an investor. You will learn about the importance of tax efficiency and how to keep more of your hard-earned money in your pocket. We will also explore the power of compound interest, a force that can significantly build your wealth over time.

This book is designed for a diverse audience. Young professionals in their 20s and 30s will find strategies to start building their retirement funds early. Meanwhile, high-income earners will discover ways to optimize their taxes and increase their net worth. Those approaching retirement age will also receive guidance on maximizing their existing savings and investments.

Throughout this book, I promise to provide practical advice and tools that are easy to follow. You will find actionable strategies and insights that can positively alter your approach to retirement planning. With clear guidance, you will be empowered to take control of your financial future.

I hope that engaging with this book will give you a new perspective on financial independence. You will find a roadmap to achieve it, equipped with the knowledge and tools needed to succeed. The path to financial security begins with understanding and implementing the concepts discussed here.

Let us set off on this experience together. With each page, you will gain the confidence to take charge of your financial future. Time waits for no one, but with the right tools and understanding, you can be ready for whatever comes your way.

Chapter 1
The Foundation of Early Planning

Retirement planning often seems like a distant concern and a task best left for the future. Yet, consider the story of one of my clients, a young professional named Alex. At 25, Alex began investing $200 monthly. He knew that small sacrifices today could yield significant rewards tomorrow. Over 40 years, with an average annual return of 7%, Alex's contributions grew to approximately $480,000—a testament to the power of compound interest.

Contrast this with Charlie, who delayed starting until age 35. Despite contributing the same $200 monthly, Charlie's investments over 30 years grew to only $240,000. By starting just 10 years later, Charlie ended up with half of Alex's total retirement fund, even though both contributed the same amount monthly.

But early planning doesn't just involve compound interest—it also involves creating financial flexibility. Alex's head start provided room for adjustments as life developed, like scaling back contributions temporarily during financial challenges or reallocating investments to align with changing goals. Meanwhile, Charlie's delay meant having to contribute more aggressively later in life to catch up, which created stress and limited their financial options.

This stark difference clearly shows the significant impact of time on financial growth and the importance of starting early. Planning ahead secures a larger retirement fund and gives you the freedom to adapt and make decisions on your terms.

The Advantage of Starting Young

One of the most overlooked merits of early investing is the financial flexibility created by regular dividends and returns. These returns can provide capital for additional investments, such as diversifying into real estate, funding a side business, or exploring higher-yield opportunities. For example, Alex, who began investing at 25, used dividends from his growing portfolio to purchase rental properties in his 40s. This boosted his passive income, broadened his insights into wealth creation, and helped him make smarter financial decisions. This kind of momentum—the ability to leverage returns to generate even more wealth—is a cycle that latecomers often miss out on, as their investments remain solely focused on catch-up growth.

Early starters create options. These options can accelerate the pace of wealth creation and offer pathways to financial independence that are unattainable for those who delay. The true power of early investing lies in the compounding of money and in the opportunities it provides. This includes the ability to pivot, reinvest, and think strategically about building a diversified and resilient financial future. For many, this is the difference between simply saving money and truly harnessing wealth creation.

Younger individuals also benefit from a greater risk tolerance. With many working years ahead, they can afford to take calculated risks in their investments without the immediate pressure of needing to cash out. Stocks and mutual funds are typically considered higher-risk assets, but they become viable options that can yield greater returns over time. This long-term horizon allows young investors to weather market fluctuations and focus on growth rather than short-term losses. Developing a solid portfolio early will allow you to set yourself up for significant financial gains as you approach retirement.

Beyond the financial mathematics, there are significant psychological benefits to starting young. Early engagement in retirement planning builds a proactive financial mindset that reduces future anxiety about financial security and instills confidence as one witnesses their wealth accumulate. This confidence reflects disciplined habits cultivated over time. With this proactive mindset comes emotional peace as the uncertainty surrounding one's financial future diminishes.

This sense of security will spill over into everyday life and improve your general quality of life. It frees you from the constant worry about money and allows you to focus on your passions, relationships, and personal growth. More importantly, though, it creates the motivation and freedom to explore opportunities you might not have considered before

—whether it's starting a business, pursuing further education, or taking calculated risks in new ventures.

These benefits lead to a totally different life path, one that breaks free from the conventional mindset of just working and saving. Instead, early investors gain a broader perspective on wealth creation and life possibilities that opens a level of confidence and ambition that sets them apart. This mindset will shift your approach to life and allow you to envision and achieve goals that many ordinary people, constrained by financial worries, never realize.

Developing financial habits is important at a young age. Consistent saving and investment practices lay the groundwork for sound financial management. Automated savings plans can facilitate this process by securing regular contributions without the need for active intervention. Budgeting for consistent investment enables you to create a stable financial routine that seamlessly integrates into your lifestyle. This disciplined approach helps avoid the pitfalls of impulsive spending and aligns everyday decisions with long-term financial goals. Through these habits, young investors like you build wealth and establish a foundation of financial literacy and responsibility that will serve them well throughout their lives (Richmond, 2023).

Interactive Element: Budgeting Exercise

I recommend establishing a monthly budget that allocates a specific percentage of your income to investments. This exercise will encourage a disciplined approach to finances. Begin by identifying your necessary expenses, then determine how much you can comfortably save each month. Aim for a minimum of 10% of your income and adjust as necessary to fit your financial situation. Use this exercise to envision your financial future and motivate consistent investment. This will reinforce the habits that will lead to long-term success (Schwahn, 2025).

The Power of Compound Interest

Compound interest is a powerful financial concept that can turn modest savings into substantial wealth over time. Unlike simple interest, which is calculated only on the principal amount, compound interest accrues on both the initial principal and the accumulated interest from previous periods. This cyclical process creates a "snowball effect," where the investment grows at an accelerating rate and leads to exponential growth. Picture a snowball rolling down a hill, gathering more snow and increasing in size as it moves. Similarly, compound interest allows your money to grow from your contributions and from the returns on those contributions. This phenomenon illustrates why Albert Einstein reportedly referred to compound interest as the "eighth wonder of the world (Mikkelson, 2006)."

Let's take a closer look at the tangible benefits of compound interest with an example. An investor starts with a modest portfolio but can see remarkable growth by reinvesting dividends and interest. This approach takes advantage of compounding because it allows the initial investment to generate ever-increasing returns. In contrast, those who withdraw returns instead of reinvesting lose out on the potential for exponential growth.

The role of time in compounding cannot be emphasized enough. It acts as the most important factor in maximizing the benefits of compound interest. The difference between 10 and 30 years of compounding is monumental. Over a decade, investments grow steadily. However, over three decades, the growth becomes exponential and turns modest initial sums into significant assets. This long-term perspective illustrates why starting early and remaining patient is so beneficial. The compounding effect rewards those who give their investments time to mature and can lead to substantial gains that might otherwise seem unattainable.

Patience and consistency are indispensable allies in the quest for maximizing compound interest benefits. Setting up automatic contributions sets you up for regular investment, and it eliminates the temptation to skip contributions when financial demands arise. This consistency allows the compounding effect to work its magic uninterrupted by market fluctuations or personal whims. Staying invested during market downturns is also important. While it may be tempting to pull out funds during turbulent times, history shows that markets tend to recover over time. Maintaining a steady course allows you to capitalize on the eventual upturns, which further supports the compounding effect (Fernando, 2024).

Setting Financial Goals in Your 20s and 30s

Establishing clear financial objectives early in life is a significant element of effective retirement planning. This stage, often marked by career beginnings and newfound independence, is the perfect time to lay a solid financial foundation. Setting realistic and measurable goals can serve as a guide that steers you toward financial security and independence. A balanced approach that differentiates between short-term and long-term goals is beneficial. For instance, a short-term goal might be saving $5,000 for a vacation in two years, while a long-term goal could involve accumulating $500,000 for retirement by age 65.

The SMART goal framework—Specific, Measurable, Achievable, Relevant, and Time-bound—offers a powerful template for creating these objectives. Consider the example of Sarah, a 25-year-old graphic designer. Sarah's long-term goal is to save for retirement. Using the SMART framework, she creates the following plan:

- **Specific:** Save $500,000 for retirement.

- **Measurable:** Contribute $200 monthly to a retirement account, earning an average annual return of 7%.
- **Achievable:** This amount is within her budget after accounting for rent, utilities, and discretionary spending.
- **Relevant:** Saving for retirement aligns with her goal of achieving financial independence and security.
- **Time-bound:** Reach $500,000 by age 65, starting immediately.

Sarah also applies the framework to her short-term goal of purchasing a car within three years:

- **Specific:** Save $15,000 for a car.
- **Measurable:** Set aside $400 monthly in a high-yield savings account.
- **Achievable:** She adjusts her entertainment budget and increases freelance work to free up this amount.
- **Relevant:** A reliable car will help her commute to work and grow her freelance business.
- **Time-bound:** Achieve the goal within three years.

By implementing the SMART framework, Sarah creates clarity around her financial objectives and builds confidence as she achieves smaller milestones along the way. This structured approach provides a clear, actionable path toward both short-term and long-term financial security (Bell, n.d.).

Prioritizing financial milestones is a significant aspect of planning in your 20s and 30s. Key milestones, such as building an emergency fund and paying off student loans, can significantly shape your financial future. An emergency fund serves as your financial safety net that offers peace of mind and security during unexpected situations like job loss, car repairs, or medical emergencies. Aim to save three to six months' worth of living expenses based on your monthly costs. To do this, start by automating savings into a high-yield savings account, where you contribute a manageable amount from each paycheck until you reach your goal (Johannen, 2023).

Balancing your savings and debt repayment is important. A good strategy is to allocate 50% of available discretionary income to your emergency fund and 50% toward debt repayment until your emergency fund reaches at least one month's worth of expenses. Once that initial milestone is met, shift more resources toward debt reduction while continuing to build your emergency fund incrementally (Bennett, 2024).

For tackling debts, consider the debt snowball or avalanche methods:

- **Snowball Method:** Focus on paying off your smallest debts first while making minimum payments on larger debts. This builds momentum and motivation as you see quick wins.
- **Avalanche Method:** Prioritize paying off debts with the highest interest rates first, minimizing the total interest paid over time. This method is more cost-effective but may take longer to see tangible progress.

Both methods are effective. I encourage you to choose the one that aligns best with your financial goals and motivation style. Strategically building your emergency fund while reducing high-interest debt will create a strong financial foundation that frees up resources for future investments and long-term growth (DeMatteo, 2020).

Tracking progress is necessary to keep you on course with your financial goals. I recommend using financial tracking apps and software to monitor your income, expenditures, and savings. These tools provide a clear view of your financial health and enable you to make informed decisions and adjust your strategies as needed. Regularly reviewing your progress helps identify areas where you may need to increase savings or cut back on spending. I would also consider setting monthly or quarterly check-ins to assess whether you are meeting your goals and make adjustments as necessary. This practice keeps you accountable and reinforces the discipline needed to achieve long-term success.

Flexibility remains a key component of effective financial goal setting. Life is unpredictable, and circumstances can change rapidly and affect your finances. While having concrete goals is important, it's also beneficial to approach them with a balanced mindset. Being strict about achieving goals is necessary for discipline, but becoming overly obsessed can lead to mental exhaustion, negativity, and a loss of motivation. This can sap your momentum and make it harder to sustain progress over time.

Viewing your financial plan as a long-term experience will help you stay motivated. A short-term, narrow-minded perspective often results in burnout and poor decisions that ultimately cause you to fail the "financial marathon." Conversely, maintaining a long-term outlook with clear goals in mind allows you to pace yourself and succeed over time. Being hasty in your approach by trying to achieve everything too quickly is one of the biggest enemies of effective long-term planning.

Reevaluating your goals annually also helps you make sure that your plan remains relevant and adaptable. Adjusting to shifts in income, career changes, or personal priorities helps you stay on track without undue stress. This adaptability keeps your financial plan aligned with your changing life goals and supports a healthier, more sustainable mindset. With patience and a long-term perspective, you can maintain momentum and ultimately achieve financial success (Schwahn, 2024).

Reflection Section

I encourage you to reflect on the financial goals you have set for yourself. Are they specific, measurable, and achievable within your current circumstances?

Consider writing down your short-term and long-term goals, along with timelines for each, using the SMART goal method. Use this exercise as a way to clarify your financial intentions and inspire a deeper commitment to achieving them. Revisit these goals regularly and allow yourself the flexibility to modify them as your situation changes. This practice sharpens your focus and reinforces your overall financial strategy.

Setting and prioritizing clear financial goals in your 20s and 30s will position you for a more secure and prosperous future. These initial steps, when combined with regular tracking and flexibility, create a resilient framework for financial planning. This framework supports your immediate needs and builds a strong foundation for long-term wealth accumulation. As you go through your early career years, these strategies will guide you toward a path of financial independence and stability. They will also prepare you to face future challenges with confidence and assurance.

Building a Retirement Vision

Imagining the life you wish to lead in retirement can be a powerful motivator for planning your financial future. Picture yourself traveling to distant lands, indulging in hobbies you never had time for during your working years, or participating in community activities that bring you joy and fulfillment. Clearly defining what your ideal retirement looks like will help you align your financial strategies with these personal aspirations.

A personalized retirement plan reflects the essence of who you are and what you value most. It doesn't just involve amassing wealth but making sure that your financial strategies align with your lifestyle goals. Whether it's pursuing art classes, engaging in volunteer work, or simply having the freedom to spend time with loved ones, a tailored plan makes sure that your financial path supports these desires. Aligning your investments and savings with your personal goals creates a coherent strategy that caters to your unique needs and aspirations. This alignment turns your financial plan into a living document that changes as you do and adapts to changes in your life while keeping your goals in sight.

However, in the pursuit of this vision, you must remain vigilant against lifestyle inflation. This is a subtle yet pervasive challenge. Lifestyle inflation occurs when increased earnings lead to proportionate increases in spending that erode potential savings and leave you with less than anticipated for retirement. The temptation to upgrade your lifestyle in response to rising income can be strong, but it is important to differentiate between needs and wants. Controlling spending growth through strategies such as adhering to a budget, setting limits on discretionary spending, and prioritizing investments over indulgences will allow you to manage lifestyle inflation and safeguard your financial future.

Let me explain this further with an example. One of my clients got a promotion with a significant pay raise. He went from earning $50,000 a year to $75,000. This increase was amazing. However, instead of putting this extra income into his savings accounts, he increased his spending habits. He bought a new car, got his family new phones, and even purchased an above ground pool. Unfortunately, he ended up regretting his purchasing decisions. He realized how much money was lost considering the compound interest it could have gained and vowed to be more careful with his income going forward.

That said, focusing solely on retirement can feel distant and overwhelming. Talking about goals decades away may make you feel like you must sacrifice the joy of the present, which understandably reduces motivation and causes procrastination. It's natural to want to enjoy the moment, especially as income increases. That's why I encourage all my clients and you as the reader to reframe retirement planning as planning for the next 10 to 15 years. For example, a 25-year-old can envision what they'd like their life to look like in their 40s. By focusing on creating the life they want just a decade or so from now, the process feels more tangible and exciting. Once they reach that milestone, they can plan for the next 10 to 15 years to maintain motivation and momentum toward retirement.

This approach allows for enjoying the present while planning for the future, and it builds financial security in achievable increments. Managing lifestyle inflation and thinking in shorter, actionable timeframes creates a balanced path that prioritizes both your present and future happiness to keep you on track toward your long-term goals.

Creating a preliminary budget is an invaluable exercise in planning for retirement. This budget serves as a financial blueprint that provides a clear picture of your expected expenses based on your current lifestyle. You can start doing this by listing your necessary monthly costs, such as housing, utilities, and groceries, alongside discretionary expenditures like dining out and entertainment. Estimate future expenses by considering potential changes in your lifestyle, such as increased travel or healthcare needs.

This preliminary budget acts as a guide that allows you to adjust your financial strategies as needed to make sure that you remain within your means while still working toward your desired retirement lifestyle. Regularly revisiting and updating this budget will help you maintain control over your finances and adapt to life's changes without losing sight of your ultimate goals (Legacy Planning, 2024).

Envisioning your retirement lifestyle is a strategic tool for planning your financial future. Creating a personalized plan that aligns with your values and aspirations sets the stage for a fulfilling and secure retirement. Guarding against lifestyle inflation makes sure that your hard-earned money works for you, while a preliminary budget provides the structure needed to work through financial uncertainties. Together, these elements form a comprehensive approach to retirement planning that empowers you to take charge of your future with confidence and clarity. As you move forward, let this vision serve as your compass that guides each financial decision with purpose and intention.

Chapter 2
Becoming an Investor, Not Just a Saver

Think of a world where your money diligently works for you, multiplying in value over time. This isn't a distant dream; it's a reality attainable through investing. Yet, many find themselves trapped in the comfort of traditional savings accounts, unaware of their limitations.

Take my client Mark as an example. He had been saving money for years, and by the time he made it into my office, he had $50,000 saved. This is an incredible feat, but there was one problem: he had the money stashed away in a regular savings account that was only earning him 1% in interest. Believe it or not, this means that Mark was actually losing money because it was decreasing in value over time the way he saved it. But we quickly fixed this issue. Together, we took that 50K and stashed it across investing, retirement, and high-yield savings accounts to make it so that his money was working for him, not against him.

As you can see, these accounts provide returns that barely keep pace with inflation, if at all. The average interest rate on these accounts lingers at around 0.05%, a stark contrast to the average inflation rate of about 2% historically. The disparity results in a gradual erosion of purchasing power and leads to a critical question: Is your money really growing, or is it losing value?

In this chapter, we'll explore the limitations of savings accounts and discuss some alternatives that will help your money grow effort-free.

The Limitations of Saving Accounts

Inflation acts silently and persistently, and it diminishes the value of money tucked away in savings accounts. Consider placing $100 in a savings account today. Twenty years later, because of inflation, that $100 might buy considerably less than it does now. Inflation reduces what your savings can actually purchase over time. This makes it important to understand that while savings accounts offer security, they do not provide the growth necessary to outpace these erosive forces. Inflation's quiet erosion demands a more proactive approach to wealth management and future planning.

Beyond inflation, the opportunity cost of not investing is significant. Funds idly sitting in savings accounts miss the chance to participate in the stock market's potential for higher returns. Historically, the stock market has offered average annual returns of about 7%, far surpassing the meager yields of traditional savings accounts. This difference in growth rates can lead to substantial gains over time, which are forgone when funds remain in low-yield accounts. Investing allows you to harness the power of compound growth, where returns generate additional returns and build wealth exponentially rather than linearly.

A shift in financial strategy is thus imperative. Instead of viewing savings accounts as vehicles for long-term wealth accumulation, consider them as tools for short-term goals and emergency funds. These accounts provide liquidity and safety for immediate needs, such as unexpected expenses or planned short-term purchases. Establishing an emergency fund in a savings account gives you access to cash when unforeseen events occur without having to liquidate investments. Similarly, setting aside funds for short-term savings goals in these accounts can offer stability without risking market fluctuations.

However, relying solely on saving without investing is a fragile strategy. If you only save money, thinking investing is too risky, your financial base is essentially zero-based, no matter how much or how long you've saved. For example, picture saving diligently for five years in a savings account to cover your children's school fees. Once the fees are paid, your account is drained, and you're back to zero and are starting your savings over from scratch. This approach is neither sustainable nor rewarding, as life entails ongoing financial demands beyond a single expense, such as healthcare, extracurricular activities, devices, or future opportunities for your children.

In contrast, investing in income-generating assets builds a financial foundation that doesn't reset to zero. Over the same five-year period, if you had invested in dividend-paying stocks, rental properties, or other income-producing assets, you would have built a steady passive income stream while preserving your principal. Plus, this income could be withdrawn for planned expenses or reinvested to grow your wealth further. The key advantage is that your financial base remains intact and provides you with flexibility and options to plan for big occasions or manage unexpected costs.

Moreover, only saving without investing leaves you with a single income stream—your job. This dependency means that if you can't work for any reason, such as illness, your income stops entirely. Your financial security becomes tethered to your ability to work and places your life within the constraints of your workplace's planning and permission. In contrast, income-generating assets are lifelong allies that create revenue regardless of your circumstances. For instance, if illness prevents you from working, your assets—whether rental properties, dividend-paying stocks, or royalties—continue producing income.

This shift means your financial foundation starts from the income your assets generate, not zero. This reassurance provides financial safety and brings you closer to financial freedom and a fulfilling retirement. Pairing short-term savings accounts with long-term income-generating investments creates a balanced and secure financial strategy that supports both your immediate needs and future aspirations (Lam, 2024).

Interactive Element: Financial Strategy Assessment

Take a moment to assess your current financial strategy. Consider listing your short-term financial goals and identifying how much of your savings are allocated toward them in traditional savings accounts. Then, evaluate whether these allocations align with your long-term objectives. Reflect on opportunities for investing a portion of your savings for greater growth. Use this exercise to identify areas where a shift from saving to investing could improve your financial outcomes (Tamplin, 2023).

Investing for Passive Income

Passive income offers a sense of financial security and flexibility that allows you to focus on other pursuits. Dividend income, for instance, comes from shares of companies that distribute a portion of their profits to shareholders. These dividends can provide a reliable source of cash flow that supplements your primary income or support your retirement. Similarly, rental income from real estate represents another form of passive income, where property ownership leads to regular earnings without the constant attention required by other ventures.

Exploring the spectrum of passive income streams reveals a range of opportunities. Dividend growth stocks are a compelling option, because they offer regular dividends with the potential for increased payouts over time. Investing in companies with a strong history of raising dividends boosts your income stream and helps align with inflation and increase purchasing power.

Real estate crowdfunding platforms provide another promising avenue for passive income. These platforms, such as Fundrise, CrowdStreet, or RealtyMogul, allow individuals to invest in real estate projects without the burdens of direct property ownership, like maintenance or tenant management. For example, you could invest in a portfolio of rental properties, commercial developments, or even fix-and-flip ventures with as little as a few hundred dollars. Pooling resources with other investors gives you access to large-scale projects and markets that might otherwise be out of reach, such as luxury apartments or high-demand office spaces. These investments often generate income through rental distributions or property appreciation to provide a diversified and balanced addition to your portfolio (Olson, 2024).

Additionally, intellectual property (IP) offers a unique and often overlooked passive income stream. Creating and licensing IP by doing things like writing a book, composing music, or developing a patented invention allows you to earn royalties over time. For instance, an author may receive a steady income from book sales, or a musician might earn royalties every time their song is streamed or used commercially. This income continues long after the initial work is completed, which makes IP an attractive option for those with creative or innovative skills.

By combining diverse streams such as dividend growth stocks, real estate crowdfunding, and intellectual property, you can build a healthy passive income portfolio that generates wealth and aligns with your interests and long-term financial goals.

Financial independence is a goal many aspire to, and building passive income streams is a key strategy for achieving it. The concept revolves around the ability to sustain your lifestyle through income generated by investments. This frees you from the need to rely solely on active employment. A widely recognized guideline for sustainable withdrawals is the 4% rule, which is based on research from the Trinity Study in 1998. It suggests that if you withdraw 4% of your investment portfolio annually, adjusted for inflation, you can maintain your lifestyle for at least 30 years without running out of money in most market conditions (Pfau, 2018).

For example, if you've built an investment portfolio worth $1 million, the 4% rule suggests you can withdraw $40,000 annually for living expenses. This rule assumes a portfolio diversified between stocks and bonds, with an average annual return of around 7% minus inflation. While not foolproof, it offers a starting framework for determining how much you need to accumulate to achieve financial independence. For instance, if you estimate your annual living expenses at $60,000, you'd need a portfolio of $1.5 million to sustain that income level using the 4% rule.

However, the success of the 4% rule also depends on factors like market performance, portfolio allocation, and personal circumstances. It shows the importance of building a strong portfolio of dividend-paying stocks, real estate investments, and other passive income sources that provide multiple streams of income to reduce reliance on withdrawals during market downturns. By planning strategically and keeping withdrawal rates sustainable, you can enjoy a fulfilling lifestyle while preserving your financial resources for the long term.

Developing a strategy for passive income involves identifying and investing in opportunities that align with your financial goals. Diversifying income sources is necessary to minimize risk and secure a stable cash flow. This might involve a mix of dividend-paying stocks, real estate investments, and other income-generating assets. Reinvesting dividends for growth is another effective tactic. Using dividends to purchase additional shares compounds your investment and improves future income potential. This reinvestment strategy can significantly increase the value of your portfolio over time, which demonstrates the power of compounding in building wealth (Gratton, 2024).

Consider Sarah, a mid-career professional and one of my clients who diversified her passive income portfolio. She allocated a portion of her savings to dividend growth stocks and selected companies with strong fundamentals and a history of increasing dividends. Additionally, Sarah invested in a real estate crowdfunding platform, where she gained exposure to commercial properties across various locations. Reinvesting her dividends and rental income allowed her to steadily grow her portfolio and eventually achieve financial independence. Sarah's approach illustrates the potential of diversified income streams and how they contribute to financial security.

The pursuit of passive income also involves creating a lifestyle that offers freedom and choice. Embracing strategies that generate income with minimal ongoing effort redirects your focus toward personal passions and goals. Whether it's spending more time with loved ones, pursuing hobbies, or traveling, passive income provides the means to live life on your terms. As you explore these opportunities, I encourage you to consider how each investment aligns with your broader aspirations to make sure that your financial strategies support the life you envision.

Strategies for Consistent Investment

The pathway to financial growth often hinges on the practice of consistent investing. This strategy involves establishing a disciplined approach that withstands the test of time. One effective method to achieve this is through dollar-cost averaging. Investing a fixed amount of money at regular intervals, regardless of market conditions, helps mitigate the impact of volatility. This approach allows you to purchase more shares when prices are low and fewer when they are high to smooth out the cost over time. Such a systematic investment plan can significantly reduce the stress of trying to time the market, which even seasoned investors find challenging. The key is to remain committed to this strategy over the long haul and let the power of compounding do its work.

Maintaining consistency in investment practices requires actionable steps that build a solid routine. Setting up automatic transfers to your investment accounts helps make sure that you contribute regularly without needing to actively decide each time. This automation builds discipline, as it removes the temptation to spend money elsewhere. Additionally, creating a monthly investment schedule can further reinforce this habit. Designating specific days for review and contribution makes investing a regular part of your financial routine, kind of like paying bills. This scheduled approach builds consistency and encourages you to assess your portfolio periodically to make sure that your investments align with your changing goals.

Despite the advantages of regular investing, several obstacles can deter individuals from maintaining this practice. Market volatility often instills fear and causes hesitation in investment decisions. It's important to understand that market fluctuations are typical and should not derail long-term plans. Historical data demonstrates that markets tend to recover and grow over extended periods. They reward those who remain steadfast during downturns. To overcome this fear, I recommend focusing on your long-term objectives rather than short-term market movements. This perspective helps maintain confidence in your investment strategy, even when the market appears turbulent.

Another common challenge is managing personal finances to prioritize investing. Limited disposable income or unexpected expenses can make regular contributions seem daunting. To address this, start by analyzing your budget and identifying areas where you can cut back. Redirecting even small amounts from discretionary spending to your investment account can make a significant impact over time. Additionally, I recommend increasing your contributions incrementally as your financial situation improves, such as after receiving a raise or paying off debt. This gradual adjustment allows you to maintain a comfortable lifestyle while prioritizing long-term financial growth.

Adopting a long-term perspective is integral to successful investing. Short-term market fluctuations can be unsettling, but it's important to focus on the broader picture. Historical market trends support the notion of long-term growth, with equity markets generally showing positive returns over extended periods. This evidence reinforces the importance of staying committed to your investment strategy, even when faced with temporary setbacks. Prioritizing your long-term goals will help you cultivate patience and resilience, which are key traits that successful investors embody. This mindset improves your financial outcomes and instills a sense of confidence and control over your financial future (Benson, 2024).

Real Estate as a Wealth Builder

Real estate has long been recognized as a formidable tool for wealth accumulation that offers both income and appreciation potential. Investing in rental properties provides a dual benefit: generating consistent rental income while the property itself appreciates in value over time. This form of investment can create a steady cash flow that serves as a reliable source to cover expenses or supplement other income streams. The tangible nature of real estate offers a sense of security, as properties can be managed and improved to increase their value and appeal. Additionally, real estate investment trusts (REITs) present an accessible option for those who prefer a more hands-off approach. By investing in REITs, you can hold a stake in a diversified portfolio of income-producing real estate that benefits from the expertise of professional management and allows you to enjoy liquidity like that of stocks.

One of the significant advantages of real estate investing lies in its ability to diversify an investment portfolio. Real estate serves as a hedge against inflation, as property values and rental income typically increase with inflationary pressures and preserve purchasing power over time. Additionally, real estate investments often have a low correlation with stocks and bonds, meaning they can provide a stabilizing effect during periods of market volatility to help mitigate overall portfolio risk.

Tax benefits further improve the appeal of real estate investing. Property owners can deduct a range of expenses from their taxable income, including mortgage interest, property taxes, insurance premiums, and operating costs such as maintenance and property management fees. One of the most valuable tax benefits is depreciation, which allows investors to deduct a portion of the property's value (excluding the land) annually as it "wears out" over time despite the property potentially appreciating in market value. For example, a residential rental property worth $275,000 (excluding land value) can be depreciated over 27.5 years in the U.S., resulting in an annual depreciation deduction of $10,000. This deduction can be used to offset taxable rental income and reduce the investor's tax liability (The Entrust Group, 2024).

Depreciation also plays a role in tax optimization, regardless of whether the property is positively or negatively geared:

- **Positive Gearing (When Rental Income Exceeds Expenses):** Depreciation helps reduce taxable income even when a property generates a profit. For example, if an investor earns $15,000 in annual rental income but has $8,000 in expenses, they would have $7,000 in taxable income. However, adding a $10,000 depreciation deduction reduces their taxable income to $0. This effectively eliminates their tax liability on the rental property while still pocketing the profit.
- **Negative Gearing (When Expenses Exceed Rental Income):** Depreciation amplifies the tax benefits of a loss-making property. For instance, if an investor has $15,000 in expenses but earns only $10,000 in rental income, they would have a $5,000 loss. Adding $10,000 in depreciation deductions increases the loss to $15,000, which can then be offset against other taxable income (like a salary), which results in a reduced overall tax burden (Waraker, 2023).

In addition to tax benefits, real estate investors can

leverage a variety of financial tools to optimize their cash flow and flexibility. For example:

- **Offset Accounts:** These accounts are linked to your mortgage and reduce the interest payable by offsetting the balance against the loan principal, saving thousands in interest over time.
- **Redraw Facilities:** These allow access to extra payments made toward a mortgage. This provides a financial safety net for emergencies or further investments (Hartstein, 2024).
- **Equity Loans:** Leveraging the equity in an appreciating property enables investors to secure funds for additional investments or renovations, which creates a compounding effect on their wealth (Kagan, 2024b).

Strategically utilizing depreciation allows investors to significantly optimize their tax position, whether they own positive or negative cash flow properties. When combined with financial tools and real estate's inherent inflation-hedging properties, these strategies create a powerful framework for maximizing both short-term cash flow and long-term wealth creation.

Entering the real estate market may seem daunting, but several strategies can facilitate a smooth transition. House hacking is a popular and innovative approach. For instance, imagine purchasing a duplex for $300,000 with a mortgage payment of $1,800 per month. By living in one unit and renting the other for $1,200 monthly, your out-of-pocket housing expense is reduced to just $600. This significantly lowers living costs and provides hands-on experience in property management, including dealing with tenants, maintenance, and budgeting. House hacking can also extend to renting out spare rooms in a single-family home, which is particularly common in high-cost areas, where every bit of extra income helps offset expenses.

Real estate syndications offer another pathway into the market, especially for those looking to participate in larger-scale investments. For example, you could consider joining a syndication deal where a group of investors pools $2 million to purchase a $10 million apartment complex. As a syndication member contributing $50,000, you gain a fractional ownership stake in the property and share in the rental income and future profits from property appreciation. The deal is typically managed by experienced professionals who handle property operations, tenant management, and financial planning, which allows you to benefit without direct involvement. Syndications provide access to commercial properties or large residential complexes that might otherwise be out of reach for individual investors. This spreads risk across a larger group while leveraging economies of scale to improve returns.

These strategies, when executed with due diligence, such as thoroughly vetting tenants in house hacking or reviewing syndication sponsor track records, can pave the way for successful real estate ventures. Starting with manageable, strategic investments will help you build confidence, generate income, and lay the foundation for a robust real estate portfolio.

Despite its potential, real estate investing is not without risks and misconceptions. Some may assume that real estate always appreciates, which neglects the cyclical nature of property markets. Understanding market cycles and timing your investments appropriately can mitigate the risk of buying at inflated prices. Additionally, effective property management is important, as it directly impacts tenant retention and property value.

Real estate investment requires a significant upfront financial commitment, which can feel daunting for investors with limited resources. This makes ongoing education about market cycles and asset types necessary for staying on track and avoiding panic during downturns. For example, understanding how residential properties perform during economic slowdowns versus how commercial spaces react can guide your decisions more strategically. Performing due diligence before acquiring a property is also beneficial. This includes assessing the property's condition, evaluating the local market, and analyzing financial projections.

To overcome these challenges with confidence, it's incredibly helpful to work with professionals such as buyer's agents, accountants, conveyancers, and home loan brokers. These experts can lead and assist you in every step of the process, from property selection and financial analysis to legal checks and securing loans. They provide peace of mind by managing complex aspects of the transaction and offer a valuable learning opportunity. Observing and working closely with these professionals will give you insights into real estate investing and equip you with the knowledge to handle similar tasks independently in the future if desired. Combining thorough preparation, expert guidance, and a commitment to ongoing learning will help you minimize risks, maximize returns, and build a successful real estate investment portfolio (Beattie, 2024).

As this chapter concludes, it's evident that real estate offers an effective approach to building wealth. By understanding its benefits, implementing strategic entry methods, and acknowledging potential risks, you can successfully integrate real estate into your investment portfolio. This chapter describes the importance of diversification and proactive management in achieving financial stability. Looking ahead, the next chapter will explore the basics of investment and guide you through the principles that will underpin your investment decisions across all asset classes and ages.

Chapter 3
Investment Basics for All Ages

Many of us have experienced standing at the crossroads of financial security and uncertainty, where the choices you make today shape the reality of your tomorrow. One of the most important decisions in this is understanding asset allocation. This is a strategy that can significantly influence your financial success. Asset allocation involves distributing your investments across various asset classes, such as stocks, bonds, and cash equivalents, to balance risk and reward.

This strategy is not a one-size-fits-all approach. It requires careful consideration of your individual circumstances, including age, risk tolerance, and financial goals. Thoughtfully diversifying your portfolio will help you mitigate potential risks while positioning yourself for growth. You'll discover everything you need to know about asset allocation, diversification, and balancing risk and reward for your investments in this chapter.

Understanding Asset Allocation

Stocks are known for their high return potential, and they often become a significant part of an investment portfolio, especially for younger investors who have a longer time horizon to weather volatility. On the other hand, bonds offer more stability and predictable income, making them an attractive option for those nearing retirement. Meanwhile, cash equivalents, such as money market funds, provide liquidity and safeguard against market downturns. However, they also typically offer lower returns. Real estate and alternative investments also play a prevalent role in asset allocation because they offer diversification and potential income streams. Combining these asset classes creates a strong financial framework that can adapt to market fluctuations and personal changes.

The factors influencing asset allocation are as diverse as the individuals making these decisions. Your age is a fundamental consideration; younger investors in their 20s and 30s can afford to take more risks and allocate a higher percentage of their portfolio to stocks. This approach capitalizes on growth potential, aiming for long-term goals like retirement. As you progress into your 40s and 50s, a balanced mix of stocks and bonds becomes prudent, as it maintains growth while introducing stability. By the time you reach your 60s, the focus often shifts toward preserving capital and generating income, with an increased allocation to fixed-income assets like bonds. This strategic shift reflects a natural progression toward a more conservative approach as retirement approaches.

Risk tolerance is another significant element in determining your ideal asset mix. Consider your comfort level with market volatility and potential losses. An aggressive investor may favor a higher allocation to stocks and embrace the potential for greater returns despite increased risk. In contrast, a conservative investor might prioritize bonds and cash equivalents because they value stability over high returns. Your financial goals also play a role. I often have clients with varied risk tolerances. At any given time, I have both young professionals trying to slowly build their wealth over time with stock investing and people approaching retirement who are looking for a faster and safer option like Roth IRAs. Everyone is different, and these personal factors create a unique financial blueprint that guides the distribution of your investments.Adjusting asset allocation over time is necessary for maintaining alignment with your changing life circumstances. Regularly reassessing your asset mix will help you make sure that it continues to reflect your current goals and risk tolerance. Rebalancing strategies, such as selling assets that have outperformed and purchasing those that have lagged, help maintain your desired allocation. The frequency of rebalancing varies, but many financial advisors recommend a review annually or when significant life events occur. This practice preserves the integrity of your investment strategy and adapts to changes in the market and your personal situation.

Several tools and resources are available to aid in determining your optimal asset allocation. Online questionnaires and calculators provide personalized insights based on your financial profile. These tools consider factors such as age, income, and risk tolerance to offer tailored recommendations for asset distribution. Additionally, consulting with a financial advisor can provide expert guidance and a deeper understanding of complex investment strategies. Leveraging these resources will give you clarity and confidence in your financial decisions and empower you to allocate your assets with assurance and precision (Chen, 2023).

Diversification: Not Putting All Eggs in One Basket

Diversification is a fundamental principle in the investment world, and it's aimed at reducing risk by spreading investments across various asset classes. This approach is often summarized by the adage, "Don't put all your eggs in one basket." By diversifying, you minimize the impact that a poor-performing investment can have on your overall portfolio. Unlike asset allocation, which focuses on the proportion of different asset classes in your portfolio, diversification emphasizes the variety within those classes. For instance, while asset allocation might determine your ratio of stocks to bonds, diversification makes sure that your stock investments are spread across different industries, geographic regions, and company sizes.

A well-diversified portfolio can mitigate losses and improve stability by providing a buffer against market volatility. Historical examples strongly support this point. During the dot-com bubble of the early 2000s, many investors concentrated heavily on technology stocks, drawn by the rapid rise of internet-based companies like Pets.com, Webvan, and others. When the bubble burst in 2001, the Nasdaq Composite Index plunged nearly 78% from its peak, which wiped out billions in wealth. Investors who had heavily allocated to tech stocks faced catastrophic losses. In contrast, those with diversified portfolios that were spread across sectors like consumer goods, healthcare, and utilities experienced far less severe declines, as the downturn in tech was offset by stability in other areas.

Similarly, during the 2008 financial crisis, portfolios concentrated in financial stocks, such as Lehman Brothers, Bear Stearns, and AIG, saw devastating losses as the housing bubble burst and the financial sector crumbled. The S&P 500 plummeted nearly 57% from its high, and financial-sector stocks were hit the hardest. However, diversified investors who held bonds, international stocks, and defensive sectors like healthcare or consumer staples saw significantly smaller losses. Bonds, in particular, acted as a safe haven, with U.S. Treasury securities rising in value as investors sought safety (DiLallo, 2024).

These examples vividly illustrate how diversification helps safeguard investments against sector-specific downturns by maintaining resilience in the face of economic uncertainty. Spreading investments across a mix of asset classes, sectors, and geographies minimizes the impact of any single market failure and helps investors weather even the most turbulent economic periods.

Achieving effective diversification requires deliberate and strategic action. One approach is to include international stocks and bonds in your portfolio. Investing globally gives you exposure to different economic growth patterns and currency dynamics, which can reduce risk and improve returns. Diversification within asset classes is also important. For stocks, this means spreading investments across various sectors, such as technology, healthcare, and consumer goods. Within bonds, consider a mix of government, corporate, and municipal bonds to balance risk and reward. This internal diversification will help you make sure that no single investment exerts undue influence over your portfolio, which builds stability and growth potential.

However, diversification efforts can be undermined by common pitfalls. Over-concentration in a single sector or geographic region is a frequent mistake. For instance, an investor enamored with the booming tech industry might allocate a disproportionate share of their portfolio to tech stocks, which inadvertently increases risk. To avoid such imbalances, regularly review your portfolio composition and adjust as needed to maintain true diversification. Another pitfall is neglecting to diversify within asset classes. This can leave your portfolio vulnerable to specific risks. For example, holding a variety of stocks that are only in large-cap U.S. companies fails to capture the benefits of smaller-cap or international stocks.

Additionally, many beginners struggle to understand the difference between interest from savings accounts and dividends or passive income generated from investments. On the surface, the numbers may seem comparable. Earning $500 in interest from a savings account might feel like receiving $500 in dividends from stocks or rental income from real estate. However, the distinction lies in the sustainability and potential for growth.

- **Interest from a savings account** is a fixed return, typically tied to the bank's rate, which often lags behind inflation. For example, if a savings account offers a 2% annual return while inflation rises at 3%, the real purchasing power of your money declines over time. Savings accounts preserve principal but do little to grow wealth.
- **Dividends or passive income from investments**, on the other hand, are tied to assets that can appreciate over time. For example, a stock that pays a 4% annual dividend may also grow in value. This creates an upward compounding effect. Similarly, rental income from a property provides steady cash flow and typically increases with inflation while the property itself appreciates.

This dynamic makes dividends and passive income inherently more sustainable and beneficial. Investments like dividend-paying stocks, real estate, or REITs generate cash flow that can be reinvested to grow your wealth further or used to cover expenses without depleting your principal. This contrasts sharply with savings accounts, where withdrawing money reduces your balance and future earning potential. For example, withdrawing $1,000 from a savings account immediately diminishes the balance and future interest. Conversely, using $1,000 from dividends doesn't impact the asset generating those dividends and allows it to continue producing income.

Understanding this difference is important for long-term financial planning. Shifting focus from fixed interest to income-generating assets safeguards against inflation and positions yourself to build sustainable wealth. Avoiding common pitfalls in diversification and embracing the value of passive income helps you create and maintain a more resilient and growth-oriented investment strategy.

Diversification is not a guarantee against loss, but it is a proven strategy for achieving long-term financial goals with minimized risk. Spreading your investments across different asset classes, industries, and regions will put you in a position to weather market fluctuations and capitalize on diverse opportunities. This approach requires vigilance and regular adjustments to make sure that your portfolio remains aligned with your financial objectives. Remember, diversification requires balance and foresight, but it also provides a foundation that supports and sustains your financial endeavors through the inevitable ups and downs of the market (Segal, 2023).

Balancing Risk and Reward

Investing is a delicate balance between risk and reward, and it's a relationship that underpins every financial decision you make. This risk-return trade-off highlights a fundamental principle: the potential for higher returns comes with increased risk. The challenge lies in using this trade-off to align with your financial goals and risk tolerance. Risk tolerance is your ability and willingness to endure market fluctuations and potential losses. Understanding your personal risk tolerance is important in shaping a portfolio you can stick with through thick and thin. Tools like risk assessment questionnaires can offer valuable insights into your comfort level with volatility that help you tailor your investment strategy accordingly.

Investment risks vary widely, and it is beneficial to recognize the different types of risks involved. Market risk, also known as systematic risk, arises from factors that affect the entire market, such as economic downturns or geopolitical events. For instance, during the 2008 financial crisis, global stock markets experienced massive declines that caused even well-diversified portfolios to lose value. This type of risk is inherent in all investments and cannot be entirely eliminated, though it can be mitigated through long-term investing and diversification.

Credit risk refers to the possibility that a bond issuer will default on its obligations and impact the return on investment. A notable example is the 2001 default of Enron, where bondholders lost much of their invested capital after the company filed for bankruptcy. Investors in corporate bonds must carefully evaluate the credit ratings of issuers to reduce this risk.

Inflation risk involves the erosion of purchasing power due to rising prices over time. For example, if you invest in a savings account with a 1% annual return while inflation rises at 3% per year, the real value of your money decreases as your returns fail to keep up with the cost of goods and services. To counteract inflation risk, investments like inflation-protected securities (e.g., TIPS) or equities with long-term growth potential are often recommended.

Liquidity risk is another significant but frequently overlooked factor. This risk arises when an investor cannot quickly sell an asset without incurring a loss. For example, owning a property in a niche real estate market can become problematic if market demand dries up and the property takes months or even years to sell. Novices regularly underestimate this risk, particularly with non-liquid investments like real estate, collectibles, or certain alternative assets.

Behavioral risk refers to the danger of making poor decisions due to emotional responses, such as panic-selling during a market downturn or greed-driven overinvestment during a boom. During the dot-com bubble, many novice investors poured money into tech stocks without proper due diligence, only to suffer massive losses when the bubble burst. This risk shows the importance of maintaining discipline and adhering to a clear investment strategy rather than being swayed by emotions or market trends.

High-risk investments, such as penny stocks or options, offer the allure of substantial gains but come with significant volatility and potential for loss. For instance, an investor who purchases penny stocks in an unproven biotech company might see dramatic price swings, and they could potentially lose their entire investment if the company fails to meet its projections. These investments require careful research and a high tolerance for risk.

Conversely, low-risk investments, like government bonds or high-yield savings accounts, provide stability and predictable returns but with limited growth potential. A 10-year U.S. Treasury bond offers a reliable income stream, though the returns are generally lower than riskier asset classes. These investments are ideal for individuals prioritizing capital preservation or nearing retirement.

Managing investment risk involves employing strategies to mitigate potential downsides while still pursuing returns. One such strategy is the use of stop-loss orders. This tool allows you to set a predetermined price at which a security will be sold automatically, which limits potential losses in a declining market. Implementing stop-loss orders can protect your investments from drastic downturns and make sure that your portfolio remains aligned with your financial objectives. Another strategy is hedging with options, which can offset potential losses in an existing investment. Options provide the right to buy or sell a security at a specified price within a set timeframe. This offers flexibility to reduce risk while maintaining exposure to potential gains.

Above all strategies, the most important and ultimate approach is to study deeply and consistently to understand the core concepts and characteristics of different asset types. Each asset type, whether stocks, bonds, real estate, commodities, or intellectual property, has unique features, strategic advantages, and associated risks. Investing successfully requires ongoing learning through studying, reading, and researching to establish a solid strategy. This includes having a clear understanding of why you are investing in specific assets and how they align with your long-term financial goals.

Knowledge is power, and the biggest risk is investing without fully understanding the assets. Blindly following advice from others or basing decisions on rumors can lead to significant losses. Investing doesn't just involve using tools like stop-loss orders or hedging. It requires you to equip yourself with the knowledge and confidence to make informed, strategic decisions. In doing so, you can work through risks effectively and build a resilient investment portfolio.

While these strategies can help manage risk, maintaining a long-term perspective is important. Market volatility is inevitable, but history shows that markets tend to recover and grow over time. The key is to remain focused on your long-term goals instead of reacting to short-term fluctuations. A long-term perspective instills patience and resilience that enables you to overcome market downturns without panic. Historical recoveries, such as the rebound following the 2008 financial crisis, illustrate the market's ability to bounce back. Staying the course positions you to benefit from the eventual upturn, which improves your potential for achieving your financial aspirations (Parker, 2023).

Introduction to Income-Generating Assets

Income-generating assets hold a significant place in any well-rounded investment portfolio. This is because they provide a steady stream of revenue that can stabilize financial plans, especially in retirement. These assets—which include dividend-paying stocks, real estate investment trusts (REITs), bonds, intellectual property, alternative investments, funds, and digital assets—contribute regular income through dividends, interest, royalties, or rental payments.

Dividend-paying stocks are shares in companies that distribute a portion of their profits to shareholders, typically on a quarterly basis. This income is a source of regular cash flow and an indicator of a company's financial health and commitment to sharing success with investors. Similarly, REITs invest in income-producing real estate and must distribute at least 90% of taxable income to shareholders annually. This provides a reliable income stream while offering exposure to the real estate market without direct ownership.

Bonds offer fixed interest payments at regular intervals and range from low-risk government bonds to higher-yield corporate bonds. These provide stability, particularly in periods of market volatility, and are an important component of a diversified portfolio.

Intellectual property (IP), such as books, music, patents, or trademarks, generates royalties over time, which offers scalable income with minimal additional effort after creation. For example, authors can earn from book sales for years while inventors collect licensing fees for patented technologies. IP income diversifies revenue streams and can grow significantly as demand for the asset increases.

Alternative investments, including peer-to-peer lending platforms and cryptocurrency staking, offer innovative ways to generate income. For instance, P2P lending connects investors directly with borrowers to earn interest without traditional financial institutions. While these options come with higher risks, they can provide attractive returns and portfolio diversification.

Funds, such as exchange-traded funds (ETFs), mutual funds with dividends, and closed-end funds (CEFs), allow investors to pool resources into diversified portfolios. Many income-focused funds emphasize dividend-paying stocks or bonds, which offer consistent payouts while spreading risk. For example, dividend-focused ETFs provide exposure to a basket of high-yielding stocks to simplify income generation for investors.

Digital and online assets have emerged as powerful income generators as well. Blogs, YouTube channels, e-commerce stores, and affiliate marketing platforms offer scalable revenue potential. For instance, a successful YouTube creator can earn through ad revenue, sponsorships, and memberships, while an e-commerce store provides income from product sales. These assets can be established alongside traditional investments to diversify and expand income sources.

The inclusion of income-generating assets in a portfolio serves to balance growth and income objectives. While growth equities may provide significant appreciation over time, their returns can be volatile. Incorporating assets that yield regular income can help you achieve a more stable and predictable financial outcome. This stability is particularly beneficial as you approach retirement, a phase where consistent income takes precedence over aggressive growth. Income-generating assets offer the dual advantage of potential capital gains and recurring income, which can be reinvested to compound gains or provide for daily living expenses. This approach mitigates the need to sell off growth assets during market downturns and preserves the overall portfolio value.

Bonds and fixed-income securities are classic income-generating investment choices because they provide interest payments at regular intervals. These instruments range from government bonds, which are low-risk, to corporate bonds that offer higher yields at increased risk. Peer-to-peer lending platforms have emerged as modern alternatives that connect investors directly with borrowers. By cutting out traditional financial institutions, these platforms can offer attractive interest rates for investors willing to assume the associated risk. Each of these options plays a unique role in diversifying income sources and boosting portfolio resilience.

Selecting the right income-generating investments involves careful consideration and thorough analysis to secure both consistent income and long-term sustainability. For dividend-paying stocks, evaluating the dividend yield, which is the annual dividends paid by a company relative to its stock price, is an indispensable first step. For instance, a company offering a 6% yield may seem attractive compared to one offering 3%, but a deeper analysis is needed to determine if the higher yield is sustainable or the result of financial distress or a declining stock price. Examining the company's dividend payout ratio can reveal whether the company is overextending itself. This indicates the percentage of earnings distributed as dividends. A payout ratio above 80% might signal potential issues, as it leaves little room for reinvestment or adjustments during economic downturns.

Investigating a company's history of dividend payments and increases over time is also important. For example, companies in the Dividend Aristocrats Index, which includes firms that have increased dividends for 25 consecutive years or more, often demonstrate financial resilience and a commitment to shareholder returns. Sectors like utilities or consumer staples are typically known for stable dividend payouts. This makes them safer options for income-focused investors.

For bonds, understanding the issuer's creditworthiness is necessary, as higher yields typically come with increased default risk. For instance, a corporate bond offering a 10% yield might seem appealing but could signal a company under financial stress. Reviewing credit ratings from agencies like Moody's, Standard & Poor's (S&P), or Fitch Ratings can help gauge the likelihood of default. AAA-rated bonds, like U.S. Treasuries, offer the highest security but lower yields, while BB or lower-rated bonds (junk bonds) carry higher risks and higher returns. Additionally, assessing interest rate sensitivity is beneficial, as bond prices typically decline when interest rates rise and affect their market value.

Beyond these metrics, I would consider the economic environment and industry-specific factors. For instance, investing in real estate investment trusts (REITs) during periods of rising interest rates requires careful analysis of the REIT's leverage and debt management, as higher borrowing costs can reduce profitability. Similarly, in peer-to-peer lending, evaluating borrower profiles and default rates on specific platforms like LendingClub or Prosper is necessary to minimize risk.

Incorporating income-generating assets into your investment strategy requires a careful and educated approach. It involves building a portfolio that aligns with your financial goals and risk tolerance. The right mix of income-generating assets can provide financial security and peace of mind that allows you to enjoy the fruits of your investments while maintaining a growth outlook. As you go through the world of investing, these assets serve as a foundation that supports your financial aspirations with consistent income and stability. Embracing this strategy is key to achieving a balanced and prosperous financial future and shows the importance of thoughtful investment decisions in wealth management (Esajian, 2022).

In this chapter, we have explored the important role of income-generating assets in securing a stable financial future. As you consider your investment strategy, remember that these assets provide regular income and offer a buffer against market volatility. Transitioning into the next chapter, we will discuss advanced financial tools and strategies to further improve your ability to plan for retirement with confidence and clarity.

Chapter 4
Advanced Financial Tools and Strategies

You can secure a financial future that meets your needs and allows you to embrace the retirement lifestyle of your dreams. With the myriad of investment options available, going through the process of investing can seem daunting. Annuities are often perceived as complex, but they are powerful tools designed to provide a steady income stream during retirement. As you get into the intricacies of annuities, you'll discover how they can turn the uncertainty of retirement into a more predictable financial experience.

The Role of Annuities in Retirement

Annuities are contractual financial products issued primarily by life insurance companies. These are specifically designed to provide regular payments to the holder, typically during retirement. They serve as a bridge between the accumulation phase of retirement savings and the distribution phase when consistent income becomes important. Annuities are usually linked to superannuation funds or retirement accounts in some countries, which makes them a popular choice for those transitioning from active employment to retirement. However, they are not offered through healthcare insurance, as their purpose is purely financial and not related to health coverage.

When you purchase an annuity, you enter into an agreement with a life insurance company. They promise to make periodic payments to you, either immediately or at some future date.

The starting age for annuities varies depending on the type and individual financial needs. For instance, immediate annuities begin payments soon after purchase. This makes them suitable for individuals in their late 50s or 60s who are ready to retire. Conversely, deferred annuities accumulate interest or investment growth over time, with payments starting at a later age, often 65 to 70. Deferred annuities are ideal for those who are still working and want to secure future income.

The amount of periodic payments depends on factors like the total amount invested, the type of annuity, and the payout terms. For example, if you purchase a fixed annuity with $200,000 at age 65, the insurer might guarantee annual payments of approximately 5% of the principal, providing $10,000 per year for the rest of your life. For variable annuities, payouts fluctuate based on the performance of the underlying investments, which offers the potential for higher returns but with greater uncertainty.

Fixed annuities offer a guaranteed payout that provides stability and predictable income, which is especially appealing for those seeking to mitigate market risks. For instance, retirees worried about volatile stock markets may use a portion of their savings to purchase a fixed annuity to secure a steady income for necessary expenses, such as housing or healthcare.

Variable annuities, on the other hand, allow your investment to grow with market performance. If the same $200,000 is invested in a variable annuity, the periodic payments could range significantly depending on market growth. While this offers the potential for higher returns, it also exposes you to market risk. This makes it better suited for retirees with a higher risk tolerance or additional income streams to fall back on.

Both types of annuities cater to different risk appetites and financial goals, so there is always an option suited to your specific needs. Annuities can be particularly advantageous when paired with other income-generating assets, such as dividend-paying stocks or bonds, to create a diversified and resilient income strategy for retirement.

The benefits of annuities extend beyond providing income; they offer a layer of financial security by guaranteeing income for life. This assurance can be invaluable for those worried about outliving their savings. Annuities act as a safeguard that provides financial peace of mind by offering a steady cash flow regardless of market conditions or personal longevity. This protection against outliving your savings allows you to focus on enjoying your retirement, free from the anxiety of financial uncertainty. Whether you choose a fixed or variable annuity, the underlying promise remains: a reliable income stream that supports your lifestyle throughout retirement.

Exploring the different types of annuities reveals a range of options tailored to diverse financial situations and preferences. Understanding the characteristics, advantages, and disadvantages of each type can help you select the best option for your retirement strategy.

- **Immediate Annuities**
  - **Characteristics**: Begin payments almost immediately after a lump-sum purchase, typically within 30 days. Payments are fixed and guaranteed for life or a specified term.
  - **Advantages:** Ideal for retirees who need a reliable income stream right away, such as covering living expenses shortly after retirement. They provide financial predictability and eliminate the risk of outliving your savings.

  - **Disadvantages:** Requires a significant upfront investment, and once purchased, the principal is typically non-refundable or illiquid. Immediate annuities offer limited growth potential since payments are fixed and not tied to market performance.

- **Deferred Annuities**
  - **Characteristics:** Accumulate value over time, with payments starting at a future date, often years or decades after the initial investment. Earnings grow tax-deferred until withdrawal.
  - **Advantages:** Offers the benefit of compounding over time. This makes it suitable for individuals in their 40s or 50s looking to secure income for later retirement. The tax-deferral feature allows growth without immediate tax implications, which can be especially valuable for high-income earners.
  - **Disadvantages:** Long waiting periods before payouts begin, which may not suit those requiring immediate income. Withdrawals before age 59½ may incur penalties and taxes.

- **Fixed Annuities**
  - **Characteristics:** Provide guaranteed payments at a fixed rate over the annuity term, unaffected by market performance.
  - **Advantages:** Predictable and stable income makes it a safe choice for risk-averse individuals, especially those in or near retirement. Fixed annuities are unaffected by market downturns, which provides peace of mind.
  - **Disadvantages:** Limited potential for growth. The fixed return may not keep pace with inflation and erode purchasing power over time.
- **Variable Annuities**
  - **Characteristics:** Allow investments in a portfolio of sub-accounts like mutual funds. Payments fluctuate based on the performance of these investments.
  - **Advantages:** Offers higher growth potential compared to fixed annuities, suitable for those with a higher risk tolerance and longer time horizons. Some variable annuities include

optional riders to guarantee minimum income or death benefits.
    - **Disadvantages:** Exposure to market risk. This means income is not guaranteed and could decrease during downturns. Typically comes with higher fees, including management costs and rider charges.
- **Indexed Annuities**
    - **Characteristics:** Payments are tied to a market index, such as the S&P 500. This offers a balance between fixed and variable annuities. They include a guaranteed minimum payout regardless of market performance.
    - **Advantages:** Potential for higher returns compared to fixed annuities while offering downside protection. Indexed annuities are ideal for those who want some market exposure without full risk.
    - **Disadvantages:** Returns are often capped or subject to participation rates, which means you may only receive a portion of market gains. Fees can reduce overall returns, and the complexity of

the product requires careful evaluation (Boyte-White, 2024).

This variety makes sure there is an annuity product to match diverse retirement objectives and financial strategies. Understanding the characteristics, benefits, and limitations of each type helps align your choice with your long-term income needs and risk tolerance to create a stable foundation for your retirement.

Selecting the right annuity requires careful consideration of several factors, as these decisions can significantly impact your financial future. Evaluating fees and surrender charges is important, as they can erode your overall returns. For example, a fixed annuity might charge a 1% annual management fee, while a variable annuity could have combined fees exceeding 2 to 3% annually when factoring in administrative charges, fund management fees, and optional riders. Additionally, many annuities impose surrender charges if you withdraw funds early. This usually starts at 7 to 10% of the withdrawal amount and decreases over a period of several years. If you decide to cash out $50,000 from an annuity with a 7% surrender charge in the first year, you'd forfeit

$3,500, which significantly reduces your available funds. Understanding these costs helps make sure that you don't face unexpected losses when accessing your investment.

Another significant factor is assessing the financial strength and reputation of the insurance company issuing the annuity. For instance, MassMutual and New York Life consistently receive A++ ratings from AM Best—this indicates exceptional financial stability and the ability to fulfill long-term obligations (Estrella, 2023). Choosing a highly rated insurer can provide peace of mind, as these companies are more likely to honor their commitments even during economic downturns. Conversely, selecting an insurer with lower ratings, such as a B rating, might expose you to greater risk if the company faces financial difficulties and could potentially jeopardize your payouts.

Lastly, I would consider whether the annuity aligns with your financial goals and timeline. For example, one of my clients was a 60-year-old nearing retirement. They benefited from an immediate annuity because this income began covering their living expenses right away. In contrast, another one of my clients was a 45-year-old who was planning for long-term retirement savings. They preferred a deferred annuity that allowed the investment to grow tax-deferred for 20 years before payouts begin. By carefully weighing fees, company reliability, and your specific needs, you can select an annuity that complements your overall financial strategy and provides you with a secure income for the future (Kurt, 2024).

Building a Bond Ladder

Picture having a financial strategy that gives you a steady income while protecting you from the ups and downs of changing interest rates. This is what a bond ladder does. A bond ladder is a way to invest in bonds that mature at different times, like steps on a ladder. Here's how it works: You buy several bonds, each with a different maturity date—some might mature in one year, others in three years, five years, and so on.

When the bond that matures first pays back your initial investment (called the principal), you can reinvest that money into a new bond at the current interest rate. This setup makes sure that you're always earning income from your bonds while also adjusting to changing interest rates over time.

For example, let's say you have $20,000 to invest. You could create a bond ladder by purchasing four $5,000 bonds:

1. A one-year bond at 3% interest
2. A three-year bond at 4% interest
3. A five-year bond at 5% interest
4. A seven-year bond at 6% interest

Each year, when one bond matures, you reinvest the $5,000 principal into a new bond with the current interest rate. If interest rates have risen, the new bond will likely offer a higher return. If rates have fallen, only a portion of your bonds are affected since the others still earn their original, higher rates.

This strategy reduces the risk of having to reinvest all your money during a time of low interest rates, which can happen if you buy bonds that all mature at the same time. It also enables you to regularly receive income from the bonds you hold, which makes a bond ladder a great option for people looking for both stability and flexibility in their investments.

There are many benefits to constructing a bond ladder. One of the most appealing aspects is the predictable income it generates. As bonds mature at regular intervals, they provide a steady stream of cash flow, which can be particularly beneficial for retirees seeking reliable income. This structure reduces reliance on the timing of interest rate changes, thereby mitigating reinvestment risk. Spreading out maturity dates allows you to reinvest maturing bonds at prevailing rates to potentially capture higher yields if interest rates rise. This flexibility keeps your portfolio responsive to market dynamics so you can capitalize on favorable conditions and cushion against adverse ones.

To construct a bond ladder, begin by selecting bonds with varying maturity dates. A typical ladder might include bonds maturing annually over a five to ten-year period. This diversification across maturities secures regular income and reduces exposure to interest rate fluctuations. When choosing bonds, I would consider a mix of both corporate and government bonds. Corporate bonds often offer higher yields, while government bonds provide greater security. This balance caters to different risk appetites and financial goals. It is important to evaluate the creditworthiness of the bond issuers, as this directly impacts the risk of default. Opting for high-quality, investment-grade bonds can minimize credit risk and give you peace of mind about the stability of your income stream.

Despite its advantages, bond ladders are not without limitations. One of the primary concerns is the credit risk associated with bonds. If an issuer defaults, the anticipated income from that bond could be jeopardized, which could potentially disrupt your overall income strategy. This risk shows the importance of thorough research and careful selection of bond issuers.

Additionally, while bond ladders provide predictability, they are not immune to the effects of inflation. Over time, inflation can erode the purchasing power of fixed income and diminish the real value of your returns. For example, if inflation averages 3% annually, a $1,000 bond payment today would only have the purchasing power of about $850 in a decade.

To counter this, I recommend incorporating inflation-protected securities into your ladder. One well-known example is the Treasury Inflation-Protected

Security (TIPS), issued by the U.S. government. TIPS adjusts their principal value based on the Consumer Price Index (CPI) to make sure that your returns rise with inflation. If you invest $10,000 in TIPS and inflation rises by 2% in a year, the principal value of your TIPS would increase to $10,200, and interest payments would be calculated based on the higher principal (Chen, 2024).

Another example is I Bonds, which are also issued by the U.S. Treasury. These bonds combine a fixed interest rate with an inflation rate that adjusts every six months to provide a dual layer of protection against inflation. For instance, an I Bond purchased with a combined rate of 6.89% would adjust its rate periodically, which keeps your returns aligned with inflation (Friedberg, 2023).

Including these securities in your bond ladder helps preserve your income's purchasing power and keeps your investments effective in the face of rising prices. Combining traditional bonds with inflation-protected securities can build a more resilient bond ladder that balances predictability with inflation protection.

Incorporating a bond ladder into your investment strategy requires thoughtful planning and execution. It involves balancing the need for stable income with the flexibility to adapt to changing market conditions. This approach empowers you to maintain a diversified portfolio that aligns with your financial goals and provides you with a reliable income stream that supports your lifestyle. As interest rates fluctuate, the staggered maturity structure of a bond ladder makes sure that your investments remain resilient and capture opportunities for growth while safeguarding against risks. This strategy, rooted in careful planning, offers a pathway to financial security and peace of mind that allows you to focus on what truly matters in life (Beers, 2024).

Understanding Life Insurance Options

Life insurance is an often-underestimated component of financial planning, but it serves as a significant pillar in securing your financial legacy and protecting loved ones from financial strain. Various life insurance products cater to different needs and stages of life, and they offer tailored solutions depending on your circumstances. Here are the three main types of life insurance plans.

- **Term Life Insurance:** This type provides coverage for a specified period, typically ranging from 10 to 30 years, and is generally the most affordable option. For instance, a 30-year-old father with two young children might purchase a 20-year term life insurance policy with a $500,000 death benefit for approximately $20 per month. This protects the financial security of their family if he passes away unexpectedly during the children's formative years. This plan covers expenses like mortgage payments, childcare, or college tuition. However, term life insurance has no cash value and expires at the end of the term, which means it's best suited for those seeking temporary protection during high-responsibility periods.
- **Whole Life Insurance:** This type offers lifelong coverage with fixed premiums and a cash value component that grows over time. A 40-year-old might purchase a whole life policy with a $250,000 death benefit and a monthly premium of $200. Over the years, this policy builds cash value that the policyholder can borrow against or

withdraw for major expenses like a child's education or retirement planning. The guaranteed death benefit provides peace of mind and makes whole life insurance ideal for individuals seeking both long-term protection and a financial asset.

- **Universal Life Insurance:** This option combines lifelong coverage with flexible premiums and death benefits. For instance, a self-employed individual in their 50s might choose a universal life policy with an adjustable death benefit of $300,000. This allows them to increase premiums during high-income years and reduce them during leaner periods. The cash value component grows based on market-linked investments or a guaranteed minimum rate, which offers the flexibility to adjust coverage as financial needs change. This makes universal life insurance particularly appealing for those with fluctuating income or complex financial goals.

Each type of life insurance presents unique advantages and trade-offs. Term life insurance is an affordable way to protect against income loss during important periods, while whole life insurance builds financial value over time and offers lifelong security. Universal life insurance, with its adaptability, provides a balance of coverage and cash value growth for those with more complicated financial needs. Selecting the right type requires evaluating your current financial situation, future goals, and priorities to make sure it aligns with your overall financial strategy.

Incorporating life insurance into retirement planning adds another layer of financial protection and peace of mind. It acts as a safeguard against unforeseen events and makes sure that your loved ones are financially secure in your absence. As an estate planning tool, life insurance offers tax-free death benefits, which can be used to cover estate taxes and preserve your wealth for future generations. This tax efficiency can significantly boost the value of your estate and provide a smooth transition of assets to beneficiaries. For those concerned about leaving a legacy, life insurance can ensure that your financial contributions to family, charities, or other causes continue beyond your lifetime.

The cash value component of life insurance policies, particularly whole and universal life, offers additional financial flexibility. As the cash value accumulates, it can be accessed through policy loans or withdrawals to provide a source of funds for various needs. Borrowing against cash value allows you to tap into your policy's accumulated savings without affecting the death benefit, which offers a cost-effective alternative to traditional loans. Moreover, this cash value can be used to supplement retirement income and provide a tax-advantaged stream of funds. This dual functionality improves the versatility of life insurance and turns it from a safety net into a beneficial financial tool. However, it's important to manage these withdrawals carefully, as excessive borrowing can reduce the death benefit and potentially lapse the policy.

Choosing the appropriate life insurance policy requires a comprehensive assessment of your financial needs and objectives. I recommend that you start by evaluating your coverage needs and consider factors such as outstanding debts, income replacement, and future expenses like education. For example, a 35-year-old working parent with a $250,000 mortgage, $50,000 in other debts, and two children who plan to attend college in 15 years will likely estimate needing a $750,000 term life insurance policy to cover all their expenses if they pass away prematurely.

Evaluating premiums and benefits is also helpful. Suppose the parent above compares a 20-year term life insurance policy with a monthly premium of $30 against a whole life insurance policy with a monthly premium of $200. While the term policy fits their current budget, they also weigh the potential long-term benefits of the whole life policy, such as building cash value for future borrowing needs. They choose the term policy for affordability because they know that they can revisit permanent coverage options as their financial situation improves.

I would also consider the policy's flexibility, especially if your financial situation is likely to change. For instance, the same parent might opt for a convertible term life insurance policy that allows them to transition to permanent coverage later without a medical exam, which offers adaptability as their needs change.

Finally, I encourage you to review the insurance company's financial stability and reputation. The parent from above researches insurers like MassMutual and New York Life, which have strong ratings from agencies like AM Best and consistently high customer satisfaction. This due diligence makes sure that the insurer is likely to fulfill its obligations over the long term.

Carefully considering factors like coverage needs, premium affordability, flexibility, and insurer reliability allows you to select a life insurance policy that meets your immediate needs and supports your broader financial strategy to secure long-term protection for your loved ones (Walrack, 2025).

Leveraging Roth IRAs for Tax Benefits

A Roth IRA stands out as a powerful tool for tax-efficient retirement savings. What makes it unique is that contributions are made with after-tax dollars. This means you pay taxes upfront on the money you deposit. In exchange, your investments grow tax-free, and withdrawals during retirement are also tax-free, provided you meet the eligibility requirements. For example, if you contribute $6,000 annually starting at age 30, and your investments grow at an average rate of 7% annually, your account could grow to approximately $600,000 by age 65—all of which you can withdraw tax-free.

The real allure of a Roth IRA lies in its promise of tax-free distributions during retirement, which can result in significant savings compared to other retirement accounts. For instance, if you're in the 25% tax bracket during retirement and withdraw $50,000 from a traditional IRA, you'd owe $12,500 in taxes. This leaves you with only $37,500. With a Roth IRA, that same $50,000 withdrawal would be entirely yours, as no taxes are due.

Another major advantage is the lack of required minimum distributions (RMDs), unlike traditional IRAs or 401(k)s, which mandate withdrawals starting at age 73. This means you can let your Roth IRA investments continue growing indefinitely to provide more flexibility in retirement. If you don't need the funds, you can leave the account untouched and allow it to grow further so you can potentially pass it on to your heirs.

The inheritance benefits of a Roth IRA are another significant advantage. Heirs who inherit a Roth IRA can withdraw funds tax-free if the account has been open for at least five years. For example, if you leave a $200,000 Roth IRA to your child, they can use the funds for their own financial needs without worrying about taxes, which creates a legacy of financial security.

By combining tax-free growth, flexible withdrawal rules, and the ability to avoid RMDs, a Roth IRA provides unparalleled advantages for long-term financial planning. Whether you're focused on maximizing your retirement income or leaving a tax-efficient inheritance, a Roth IRA offers benefits that are difficult to match with other retirement accounts.

Eligibility to contribute to a Roth IRA hinges on income limits, which vary based on your filing status. For 2024, single filers with a modified adjusted gross income (MAGI) below $146,000 can contribute the maximum amount, while married couples filing jointly face a threshold of $230,000. Contribution limits are set at $7,000 annually for those under 50, with an additional $1,000 catch-up contribution available for individuals 50 and older. These limits encourage consistent saving while allowing older individuals nearing retirement to bolster their accounts. Understanding these thresholds and limits helps make sure you maximize your

Roth IRA contributions without exceeding allowable amounts (Internal Revenue Service, n.d.).

Strategically using a Roth IRA within your retirement planning can significantly improve your financial outlook. One powerful strategy involves Roth conversions, where assets from a traditional IRA or 401(k) are transferred into a Roth IRA. This strategy requires paying taxes on the converted amount now, but the benefit lies in enjoying tax-free growth and withdrawals in the future. The timing of these conversions is important for minimizing tax burdens and maximizing long-term gains.

For instance, consider one of my clients, a 55-year-old individual named Alan who recently retired and has a lower taxable income because they are no longer earning a salary. However, he has not yet started taking Social Security or required minimum distributions (RMDs). This period of lower income presents an ideal opportunity for Roth conversions, as Alex can convert $50,000 per year from a traditional IRA to a Roth IRA and stay within a low tax bracket (e.g., the 12% bracket). By spreading conversions over several years, Alex avoids moving into a higher tax bracket and reduces the overall tax cost of the conversion.

Alternatively, if Alex were to wait until age 73 when RMDs are required, he might face significantly higher taxes because the RMDs, combined with Social Security benefits and other income, could push them into a higher tax bracket. Acting strategically during the "gap years" of lower income allowed Alex to maximize the benefits of the Roth conversion while minimizing taxes.

In addition to the tax advantages, Roth IRAs serve as excellent estate planning tools. Because Roth IRAs do not require RMDs during the account holder's lifetime, the funds can continue to grow tax-free. This allows for the accumulation of wealth that can be passed on to heirs. For example, if Alex leaves a $500,000 Roth IRA to his child, the child can withdraw funds tax-free over a 10-year period under current inheritance rules to preserve more of the account's value for future use.

Carefully timing Roth conversions and incorporating them into your overall financial plan can help you optimize both your tax strategy and retirement savings. This approach makes sure that you enjoy tax-free income during retirement and leave a significant tax-efficient legacy for your heirs.

When it comes to managing Roth IRA withdrawals and conversions, careful planning is necessary. Timing your conversions can lead to significant tax savings. Converting during years of lower income or after retirement, when your tax rate might be lower, can minimize the tax impact. Additionally, avoiding penalties on early withdrawals is important. While contributions can be withdrawn at any time without penalty, earnings are subject to a five-year waiting period. Make sure you meet this requirement to avoid unexpected taxes and penalties.

In the broader context of retirement planning, Roth IRAs represent a powerful tool that aligns with the goals of financial independence and tax efficiency. Integrating Roth IRAs into your strategy will allow you to leverage their unique benefits to secure a more flexible and tax-advantaged future. This approach improves your financial portfolio and provides peace of mind, knowing that your retirement funds are optimized for growth and protection (Elly, 2024). As we transition to the next chapter, we will explore how to optimize your tax strategies further to make sure your finances are both prosperous and secure.

Chapter 5
Tax Optimization Techniques

Doing your taxes can feel overwhelming, but mastering this aspect is necessary for financial success. A significant part of tax planning involves understanding tax-deferred accounts and their role in retirement savings. With these, you can harness the power of time to grow your wealth, where the government acts as a silent partner and allows your investments to compound without immediate tax burdens.

Take, for instance, my client Tina. She really struggled with optimizing her taxes as she settled into retirement. Now, instead of filing her W-2s, she needed to file taxes on money she received from her social security benefits and retirement accounts. We worked on her taxes together and discovered that she wasn't utilizing tax-approved accounts as much as she could be. Thankfully, we put a stop to that issue by coming up with some other tax optimization strategies that could help her save as much money as possible and secure a comfortable retirement for years to come.

Tax-approved accounts serve as incentives for individuals to prioritize retirement saving, and they offer a structured way to reduce taxable income and build investment growth. In this chapter, you'll learn more about tax-deferred accounts and other tax optimization strategies, like optimizing your tax credits, working with different tax brackets, and utilizing smart withdrawal strategies.

Tax-Deferred Accounts Explained

Tax-deferred accounts, such as 401(k) plans and traditional individual retirement accounts (IRAs), are designed to defer taxes on contributions and investment earnings until withdrawal, which is typically during retirement. This deferral allows your investments to grow more quickly, as the funds remain untouched by taxes until they are withdrawn. In a 401(k) plan, contributions are made pre-tax. This reduces your taxable income for the year and provides an immediate tax break. Employers often boost the appeal of 401(k) plans by offering matching contributions, usually up to a certain percentage of your salary, which can significantly boost your retirement savings. Traditional IRAs operate similarly. They allow contributions to be deducted from your taxable income, thereby lowering your current tax obligations.

The impact of tax deferral on savings growth is significant. Postponing taxes allows your investments to compound more effectively and leads to significantly larger savings over time. Consider a scenario where you contribute $5,000 annually to a tax-deferred account, such as a 401(k), over 30 years. Assuming an average annual return of 7%, your account would grow to approximately $510,000 by retirement.

If this same $5,000 contribution were made to a taxable account, with taxes on annual gains averaging 15%, your account would grow to only about $410,000. The $100,000 difference highlights how tax deferral allows your money to grow uninhibited and maximizes the effects of compounding interest over time.

The power of tax deferral lies in keeping more of your earnings invested and compounding year after year rather than losing a portion to taxes annually. By the time you reach retirement, this substantial accumulation of wealth can provide a stable financial cushion that covers living expenses, healthcare, or other unforeseen costs.

This scenario describes the importance of maximizing contributions to tax-deferred accounts. The combination of compounding growth and tax deferral serves as a powerful catalyst for building a strong financial future, and it offers peace of mind and financial security as you approach retirement. Leveraging these accounts as part of your comprehensive retirement strategy can make a significant difference in achieving your long-term financial goals.

However, it is important to be aware of the rules and limitations governing tax-deferred accounts. Contribution limits for 401(k) plans and traditional IRAs are set annually by the IRS and can vary based on age. For example, in 2025, the contribution limit for a

401(k) is $23,500, with an additional catch-up contribution of $7,500 for those aged 50 and over (Internal Revenue Service, 2024a). Traditional IRAs have a lower contribution limit, capped at $7,000, with a catch-up contribution of $1,000 for individuals over 50 (Internal Revenue Service, 2024c). Moreover, tax-deferred accounts are subject to required minimum distributions (RMDs) once you reach age 73, and these distributions are generally taxed at your ordinary income rate. Failing to take RMDs can result in significant penalties, which shows the importance of understanding these requirements to avoid unintended tax consequences.

Tax-deferred accounts can be particularly advantageous during high-earning years when reducing your current taxable income is a priority. For example, if you're in the 24% tax bracket, contributing $10,000 to a 401(k) reduces your taxable income by $10,000, which saves you $2,400 in taxes this year. This immediate tax break can be a significant benefit, especially for those in higher tax brackets during their working years. Employers often improve the appeal of 401(k) plans by offering matching contributions. For instance, if your employer matches 50% of contributions up to 6% of your salary and you earn $80,000, contributing $4,800 to your 401(k) earns you an additional $2,400 in employer matches. This effectively boosts your retirement savings.

On the other hand, traditional IRAs offer similar tax-deferred growth but are typically better suited for individuals who don't have access to an employer-sponsored plan or need additional retirement savings options. Contributions to a traditional IRA may be tax deductible, which lowers your current tax obligations (Hayes, 2023).

Comparing Roth IRAs and Tax-Deferred Accounts

While Roth IRAs provide tax-free withdrawals in retirement, they require you to pay taxes on contributions upfront. For example, if you contribute $6,000 to a Roth IRA in the 24% tax bracket, you'll pay $1,440 in taxes on that contribution now. However, all future earnings and withdrawals are tax-free. This makes it a powerful tool for those expecting to be in a higher tax bracket during retirement or who want to avoid required minimum distributions (RMDs).

In contrast, 401(k)s and traditional IRAs provide the greatest benefit if you expect to be in a lower tax bracket during retirement. For instance, if you contribute $10,000 to a 401(k) today and your tax bracket drops from 24% to 12% in retirement, you'll pay $1,200 in taxes on withdrawals. This saves you money compared to the upfront taxes on a Roth IRA (Investopedia, 2024).

Interactive Element: Personal Tax-Deferred Account Review

Take a moment to examine your tax-deferred accounts. Assess whether you are maximizing your contributions, including any employer matches. Then, review the current rules regarding RMDs and make sure that your retirement strategy accommodates these requirements. Regularly evaluating your tax-deferred accounts will help keep them aligned with your financial goals and optimize their benefits for your retirement planning.

Smart Withdrawal Strategies

When approaching retirement, the strategy behind withdrawing funds from your accounts becomes extremely important. Creating a smart withdrawal plan can significantly impact your overall tax liability and the longevity of your savings. Sequencing withdrawals strategically allows you to manage your tax brackets and extend the life of your retirement portfolio. The goal is to minimize taxes while maximizing the efficiency of your withdrawals. For instance, consider drawing funds from taxable accounts first. This approach allows your tax-deferred accounts to continue growing without the immediate tax burden. By utilizing taxable accounts initially, you take advantage of lower capital gains taxes, especially if these investments have been held for over a year. This method optimizes tax efficiency and makes sure that your tax-advantaged accounts remain untouched to preserve their growth potential for future use.

Roth conversions add another layer to your withdrawal strategy, offering a pathway to tax-free income in retirement. By converting traditional IRA funds to Roth IRAs, you pay taxes on the converted amount now, allowing for tax-free withdrawals later. This strategy is particularly beneficial if you anticipate being in a higher tax bracket during retirement. Timing these conversions is key. Consider years when your taxable income is lower, such as early retirement or periods of reduced earnings, to minimize the tax impact. By spreading conversions over several years, you can avoid pushing yourself into a higher tax bracket, effectively managing your tax obligations while securing a source of tax-free income for the future. This approach provides greater financial flexibility and aligns with long-term planning goals, ensuring that you maintain control over your retirement funds.

Tax diversification improves the flexibility of your withdrawal strategy by maintaining a mix of tax-deferred, tax-free, and taxable accounts. This balance allows you to adjust withdrawals based on your current tax situation, which optimizes tax efficiency. For example, during high-tax years, you might rely more on Roth accounts for tax-free income, while in lower-tax years, you could draw more from tax-deferred accounts to minimize the overall tax burden. This approach makes sure that you can adapt to changing financial circumstances and leverage the advantages of each account type to maximize your net income.

Tax diversification also provides a layer of protection against potential tax law changes. For instance, consider the historical shift in tax brackets under the Tax Cuts and Jobs Act (TCJA) of 2017, which reduced federal income tax rates. This is set to expire in 2025. If these rates revert to pre-2017 levels, retirees relying heavily on tax-deferred accounts for withdrawals could face higher tax bills (Tax Policy Center 2024). A well-diversified portfolio that includes Roth IRAs or taxable accounts could allow you to adjust your withdrawal strategy by drawing more from tax-free or already-taxed sources to avoid higher taxes.

Additionally, there have been discussions about eliminating the "step-up in basis" rule for inherited assets or increasing required minimum distributions (RMDs) from tax-deferred accounts. If such changes occur, having taxable or tax-free accounts could give you the flexibility to reduce reliance on accounts affected by the new rules to preserve your wealth for both retirement and legacy planning.

Diversifying across tax-deferred, tax-free, and taxable accounts positions you to work through unexpected tax law changes with confidence and make sure that your retirement strategy remains resilient and adaptable. This approach minimizes your tax burden and protects your financial stability during changing legislation.

Efficient withdrawal sequencing requires careful planning and execution. By drawing from taxable accounts before tax-deferred ones, you can take advantage of lower tax rates on capital gains and preserve the tax-advantaged growth of your retirement accounts. This approach also aligns with the strategy of using Roth accounts for tax-free income in years when your taxable income is higher. Balancing these withdrawals allows you to maintain a steady income stream while minimizing your overall tax burden. Implementing these strategies involves considering various factors, such as your current tax bracket, anticipated income needs, and the potential impact of required minimum distributions. Staying informed and proactive will optimize your withdrawals to preserve your savings and improve your financial security throughout retirement (Royal, 2025).

Tax Credits and Deductions You Need to Know

Understanding tax credits can significantly lighten your tax burden and improve your financial health. Among the most impactful is the Retirement Saver's Credit, also known as the Savings Contributions

Credit. This tax benefit is designed to encourage low-to-moderate-income earners to save for retirement. If you contribute to a retirement account like a 401(k) or IRA, you could receive a tax credit of up to $1,000 for individuals or $2,000 for married couples filing jointly. For example, if you're eligible and owe $1,500 in federal taxes, this credit could reduce your tax bill to $500. Unlike a deduction, which lowers your taxable income, this credit directly lowers the amount of tax you owe. This makes it a valuable way to save money while building your retirement nest egg. Eligibility depends on your income and filing status. In 2024, single filers must earn less than $38,250, and married couples filing jointly must earn less than $76,500 to qualify (Internal Revenue Service 2024b).

Another powerful tax tool is the Earned Income Tax Credit (EITC), which is aimed at providing financial relief to working individuals and families with low-to-moderate incomes. The EITC is especially beneficial for families with children, as the credit amount increases with the number of dependents. For example, a single parent with two children earning $25,000 could qualify for an EITC of over $6,000, depending on the year's limits. What's more, the

EITC can result in a significant refund even if you owe no taxes. This means the IRS could send you money back.

Understanding these credits and their eligibility criteria can lead to significant tax savings. For instance, combining the Saver's Credit with the EITC could result in a lower tax bill and a substantial refund. This boosts both your current financial situation and long-term retirement savings. These tax credits highlight the importance of informed financial planning and the potential benefits of exploring all available options.

For retirees, leveraging IRS-approved tax deductions can play a significant role in minimizing taxable income and maximizing financial flexibility. Medical expenses, which often form a significant portion of a retiree's budget, are one such deduction. The IRS allows you to deduct unreimbursed medical expenses that exceed 7.5% of your adjusted gross income (AGI). For example, if your AGI is $50,000, you can deduct qualified medical expenses that exceed $3,750. This deduction applies to a wide range of expenses, including doctor visits, prescription medications, dental care, hearing aids, and even long-term care services. This is as long as they are not reimbursed by insurance. Planning for large medical expenses in a single year can help you maximize this deduction by surpassing the 7.5% threshold.

Charitable contributions also offer retirees a meaningful way to reduce taxable income while supporting causes they care about. The IRS allows deductions for cash donations, the value of donated goods, and certain expenses related to volunteering, such as travel costs to a charitable event. This means if you donate $1,000 to a qualified nonprofit and also volunteer, incurring $200 in travel expenses, you could deduct both amounts to reduce your taxable income by $1,200. Retirees over age 70½ can also make Qualified Charitable Distributions (QCDs) directly from their IRA accounts, which count toward their required minimum distributions (RMDs) but are not taxable as income. This makes it a powerful tax-saving strategy.

Keeping detailed records is necessary to make sure you qualify for these deductions. For medical expenses, retain receipts, invoices, and insurance statements to document your costs. For charitable contributions, save acknowledgments from the organization and records of expenses incurred. The IRS has specific requirements for large donations, such as the rule that cash contributions exceeding $250 require written confirmation from the nonprofit.

Understanding and utilizing these IRS provisions can help retirees significantly reduce their taxable income and free up more resources for living expenses, travel, or other financial priorities. Regularly reviewing tax rules and consulting with a tax professional can help make sure that you take full advantage of these opportunities.

Maintaining accurate financial records is beneficial for claiming eligible credits and deductions. Organizing receipts and documentation is the first step in this process. Store all relevant documents, such as donation receipts and medical bills, in a systematic manner that allows for easy access during tax preparation. You could also consider using digital tools or tax software to categorize and track expenses throughout the year. These technologies simplify the record-keeping process and provide reminders for upcoming filing deadlines and potential deductions you might overlook. Staying organized helps you make sure that you can substantiate claims and maximize your tax benefits while also providing a seamless and stress-free tax filing experience.

It's also important to stay informed about potential changes in tax laws that could affect available credits and deductions. Tax regulations can change annually, which impacts eligibility and the amount of credits and deductions. Monitoring IRS announcements and updates is a proactive way to remain current on these changes. Additionally, consulting with tax professionals on an annual basis can provide personalized guidance tailored to your financial situation. These experts can offer insights into upcoming tax legislation and suggest strategies to adapt your financial plans accordingly. Engaging with professionals keeps you compliant with tax laws while optimizing your financial strategy to maximize savings. This vigilance protects your financial interests and improves your ability to work with the tax system with confidence and clarity (Steber, 2024).

Working With Different Tax Brackets

Understanding how tax brackets work is necessary for optimizing your financial strategy. The U.S. tax system operates on a progressive scale, meaning that income is taxed at increasing rates as it rises. This system comprises several brackets, each with its own marginal tax rate. The marginal rate applies only to income within that bracket, not to your entire income.

For instance, consider a single filer in 2024 with a taxable income of $50,000. The U.S. federal income tax brackets for single filers are as follows:

- 10% on income up to $11,000
- 12% on income between $11,001 and $44,725
- 22% on income above $44,725

In this case, the individual pays:

- 10% on the first $11,000, which equals $1,100
- 12% on the income from $11,001 to $44,725, which equals $4,047
- 22% on the income from $44,726 to $50,000, which equals $1,162

The total federal tax owed is $1,100 + $4,047 + $1,162 = $6,309.

While the marginal tax rate for this individual is 22% (the rate applied to the last dollar of income), their effective tax rate is lower. To calculate the effective tax rate, divide the total taxes paid by the total income:

$6,309 ÷ $50,000 = 12.62%.

This means that, on average, only 12.62% of their income is going toward federal taxes, even though their marginal rate is 22%.

Understanding this distinction is important for making informed financial decisions. For example, knowing the effective tax rate can help you determine how much of your income is actually available for savings or investments. Meanwhile, understanding the marginal rate is necessary for evaluating the tax impact of earning additional income, such as from a bonus or side job.

Managing income within tax brackets requires thoughtful planning to avoid unnecessary tax burdens. One common challenge is "bracket creep," which happens when a raise, bonus, or other increase in income pushes you into a higher tax bracket and causes you to pay a higher rate on the portion of income above the threshold. While this doesn't mean all your income is taxed at the higher rate, it can still increase your overall tax liability.

For example, picture that you are a single filer earning $44,000 annually, putting you just below the 22% tax bracket threshold in 2024. If you receive a $2,000 year-end bonus, $1,275 of it would be taxed at 12%, and the remaining $725 would be taxed at 22%, which raises your overall tax bill (Kagan, 2024c).

Strategies to Manage Bracket Creep

1. **Income-Smoothing:** Spread income over multiple years to avoid a sudden spike in taxable income. For instance, if you are self-employed and anticipate earning $55,000 this year and $45,000 next year, you could delay sending invoices or receiving payments for $5,000 until January of the following year. This keeps you within the lower tax bracket for this year while deferring some income to the next year.
2. **Timing Income Recognition:** Adjust when you receive income to control your tax liability. For example, if you're an employee who expects to be just over the 22% tax bracket threshold due to a year-end commission, you could ask your employer

to delay the payment until January. This effectively pushes that income into the following tax year, when your total earnings might be lower.

3. **Contributing to Tax-Advantaged Accounts:** Use contributions to a 401(k) or Traditional IRA to lower your taxable income. If you're nearing the 22% tax bracket and contribute $3,000 to a 401(k), that amount reduces your taxable income and potentially keeps you in the 12% bracket (Medina, 2023).

Implementing these strategies can optimize your tax liability so you can keep more of your earnings and manage cash flow more effectively. Bracket-based tax planning offers additional avenues for minimizing tax exposure. Splitting income with a spouse is one such method. Allocating income between spouses allows you to take advantage of lower combined tax rates. This is especially useful when one spouse earns significantly more than the other. Shifting income can be achieved through spousal IRA contributions or investments in joint accounts. Additionally, adjusting deductions can help maintain income within desired brackets. Deductions for retirement contributions, mortgage interest, or medical expenses can lower taxable income and keep you in a favorable bracket. Regularly reviewing and adjusting your deductions makes sure that you remain in control of your tax situation so you can make the most of your opportunities to reduce taxable income.

Shifts in tax brackets can significantly influence retirement planning, which highlights the need for proactive strategies. Anticipating changes due to life events, such as retirement, marriage, or the sale of major assets, is beneficial. These events can alter your income and tax liabilities and require adjustments in your financial plans. For instance, retiring may lower your income and place you in a lower bracket. This shift could present an opportunity to convert traditional IRA funds to a Roth IRA at a reduced tax rate. Similarly, if you anticipate an increase in income, perhaps from a pension or annuity, you could adjust your withdrawal strategy from retirement accounts to manage tax impacts. Anticipating these shifts will help you make informed decisions that optimize your tax situation and improve your financial security.

Understanding and working with tax brackets is integral to effective financial planning. Grasping the nuances of marginal and effective tax rates, employing income-smoothing strategies, and leveraging bracket-based planning techniques can minimize your tax liabilities and maximize your income. These strategies require regular review and adjustment as your financial situation changes. These concepts will serve as foundational tools and guide you toward a more secure and prosperous future as you plan your finances. Each decision, whether about timing income or adjusting deductions, plays a significant role in shaping your finances and making sure that you stay in control of your financial destiny (Garrido, 2024).

With this understanding of tax brackets and their implications, we prepare to explore the next chapter, which focuses on healthcare and long-term care planning. This transition highlights the interconnectedness of financial planning aspects, where tax strategies and healthcare decisions jointly influence your retirement readiness.

Chapter 6
Healthcare and Long-Term Care Planning

Figuring out healthcare in retirement can feel daunting, but it isn't an experience you need to take alone. I know that I felt my own fair share of anxiety when I was trying to figure out which Medicare plan would work best for me. But with a little research and some careful planning, I was able to determine that the Medicare Advantage plan was the right fit for me. It covered my basic medical, dental, and vision expenses. Plus, I was easily able to include Part D of the plan and get my prescriptions covered as well.

Medicare, the federal health insurance program, was designed to benefit those aged 65 and older. It provides indispensable coverage at a time when healthcare needs often intensify. Understanding how Medicare works, from its foundational parts to its costs and enrollment, is important. This chapter will illuminate these elements to help you make informed decisions that align with both your health needs and financial circumstances.

Medicare: What You Need to Know

Medicare is structured into four distinct parts, each addressing specific healthcare needs. Understanding these parts allows you to tailor your coverage to suit your health needs and preferences:

Part A: Hospital Insurance

- Covers inpatient hospital stays, skilled nursing facility care, hospice, and some home health care services.
- Typically premium-free for individuals who have paid Medicare taxes for at least 10 years (or 40 quarters).
- Example: If you're hospitalized for surgery, Part A helps cover the hospital room, meals, and certain medical services during your stay.

Part B: Medical Insurance

- Covers outpatient care, preventive services, ambulance services, and some home health care.
- Requires a monthly premium, which varies based on income.
- Example: If you visit your doctor for a routine checkup or need an X-ray, Part B helps cover those costs.

Original Medicare (Part A + Part B)

- Together, Parts A and B form the foundation of Medicare coverage. This is often referred to as Original Medicare.
- It does not cover additional benefits like vision, dental, or hearing services.

Part C: Medicare Advantage

- Offered through private insurers and bundles Parts A and B coverage. It typically includes additional benefits such as vision, dental, hearing, and fitness programs.

- Many Medicare Advantage plans also include Part D prescription drug coverage.
- Example: A Medicare Advantage plan may cover your annual dental cleaning, eyeglasses, and gym membership, which are services not included in Original Medicare.

Part D: Prescription Drug Coverage

- Standalone plans are available to those with Original Medicare or included in Medicare Advantage plans.
- Covers prescription medications based on the specific formulary of the chosen plan.
- Premiums vary by plan and medications covered. Example: A Part D plan might cost $30 per month but may significantly reduce the cost of expensive medications like insulin (Medicare, n.d.).

Each part serves a unique purpose and helps make sure that a comprehensive range of healthcare needs is met. For example, retirees needing frequent prescriptions might prioritize adding a Part D plan or choosing a Medicare Advantage plan that includes drug coverage, while those preferring flexibility may stick with Original Medicare and supplement it with a Medigap plan.

Eligibility for Medicare generally begins at age 65, although certain younger individuals with disabilities or specific conditions may qualify earlier. The Initial Enrollment Period (IEP) is a seven-month window that starts three months before your 65th birthday month and ends three months after. Enrolling during this period helps you avoid late enrollment penalties and gaps in coverage. Special Enrollment Periods (SEPs) offer additional opportunities to enroll or make changes under specific circumstances, such as losing employer coverage. Missing these periods can result in higher costs and limited coverage options. This makes timely enrollment extremely important.

Understanding the costs associated with Medicare is necessary for financial planning. While Part A is often premium-free, Part B requires a monthly premium, which can increase based on income. Additionally, Part B has an annual deductible and coinsurance. This means you pay a percentage of the cost for services after meeting the deductible. Part D plans also come with premiums, deductibles, and copays, which add to the overall cost. Supplementary insurance options like Medigap can help cover some of these out-of-pocket expenses and fill some gaps in Original Medicare coverage. However, Medigap policies require additional premiums and can vary significantly in cost and coverage.

Choosing the right Medicare plan involves evaluating both coverage networks and financial implications. You can start doing this by assessing your healthcare needs while considering current and anticipated medical services. Evaluate coverage networks to make sure that your preferred doctors and hospitals are included. Also, consider out-of-pocket maximums, which cap the amount you pay for covered services each year. Lower maximums can protect against high medical costs and offer peace of mind in the face of unexpected health issues. Balancing these factors helps ensure your Medicare plan aligns with your health requirements and financial situation (Lockett, 2020).

The Importance of Long-Term Care Insurance

Long-term care insurance is a beneficial financial safeguard that protects individuals from the staggering costs associated with extended care needs. This type of insurance covers expenses that arise when one requires assistance with daily living activities, such as bathing, dressing, and eating, often necessitated by aging, illness, or disability. Unlike traditional health insurance, long-term care insurance specifically addresses services like assisted living facilities, in-home care, and nursing homes. With nearly 70% of individuals over the age of 65 requiring some form of long-term care during their lifetime, planning for these potential costs is indispensable to preserving financial stability and independence.

Determining the optimal time to purchase long-term care insurance involves a strategic evaluation of both age and health. Generally, purchasing a policy in your 50s or early 60s can strike a balance between securing affordable premiums and optimizing eligibility, as waiting until later in life typically results in higher costs or denial of coverage due to health issues. Premiums are typically lower when you are younger and healthier, which makes early acquisition more financially viable. However, it is also important to consider your overall financial situation, including the ability to afford premiums over the long term, as discontinuing a policy due to financial strain can negate its benefits.

Exploring the various policy options and features available in long-term care insurance is key to tailoring coverage to meet specific needs. Policies can vary greatly, with some offering comprehensive coverage for a wide range of services while others focus on specific types of care. A significant feature to consider is an inflation-protection rider, which adjusts benefits to keep pace with the rising costs of care. Without this rider, the value of your policy may diminish over time. Additionally, understanding benefit triggers is beneficial. Benefit triggers determine when you can begin receiving benefits. Common triggers include the inability to perform a certain number of daily living activities or the need for substantial supervision due to cognitive impairment. The elimination period is the waiting time before benefits commence, typically ranging from 20 to 100 days. Opting for a shorter elimination period may increase premiums but provide quicker access to benefits, which can be indispensable in times of need.

Misconceptions about long-term care insurance often deter individuals from pursuing this valuable coverage. A prevalent misunderstanding is that Medicare will cover all long-term care needs. However, Medicare provides limited coverage and focuses primarily on short-term skilled nursing or rehabilitation services instead of ongoing custodial care. Concerns about cost can also be a barrier that prompts some to overlook the potential financial devastation of long-term care expenses. Hybrid policies, which combine life insurance with long-term care coverage, offer a solution by providing benefits even if long-term care is never needed. These policies make sure that your premiums are not wasted, as the life insurance component remains intact, which delivers a financial benefit to beneficiaries.

Knowing the limitations of Medicare and the potential costs of care allows you to make informed decisions about your coverage needs. Long-term care insurance represents a strategic investment in your future that offers peace of mind and financial protection at a time when you may be most vulnerable. Engaging with financial advisors or insurance professionals can further clarify options and tailor policies to align with your personal circumstances and goals. This will help you make sure that you are adequately prepared for whatever the future may hold (Painter, 2021).

Planning for Healthcare Costs

Estimating future healthcare expenses is a significant component of retirement planning. As you project these costs, consider the impact of inflation and potential health changes over time. Historical trends reveal that healthcare costs have consistently outpaced general inflation rates, which makes it necessary to account for these increases in your planning. To do this, begin by reviewing your current healthcare expenses, then apply an annual inflation rate of approximately 5% to estimate future costs. This approach provides a realistic framework for anticipating the financial demands of healthcare during retirement. Additionally, I would consider your personal health history and any hereditary conditions that may affect future medical needs. Incorporating these factors will create a more accurate forecast that allows you to allocate resources effectively and avoid unexpected financial burdens.

Health Savings Accounts (HSAs) offer a tax-efficient means to save for healthcare expenses by providing a triple tax advantage. Contributions to an HSA are tax-deductible, which reduces your taxable income for the year. The funds within the account grow tax-deferred, and withdrawals for qualified medical expenses are tax-free. This combination makes HSAs an attractive option for managing healthcare costs. To utilize an HSA, you must be enrolled in a high-deductible health plan (HDHP). The IRS sets annual contribution limits, with 2024 allowing up to $3,850 for individuals and $7,750 for families. Those aged 55 and older can contribute an additional $1,000 as a catch-up contribution. Eligible expenses include deductibles, copays, prescriptions, and even some vision and dental care. Maximizing contributions to your HSA enables you to secure a cushion for future healthcare needs and enjoy significant tax savings (Kagan, 2024a).

To manage and reduce out-of-pocket healthcare expenses, I recommend implementing several actionable strategies. First, I would prioritize preventive care services, such as regular check-ups and screenings, to catch potential health issues early and reduce the need for more extensive treatments. Many insurance plans offer these services at no extra cost, which makes them an effective way to maintain health and manage expenses. Additionally, I encourage you to explore medical tourism for elective procedures. Some countries offer high-quality medical care at a fraction of the cost found domestically. This allows you to access the care you need without draining your savings. Researching reputable facilities and making sure they meet international standards can provide peace of mind and substantial savings.

Integrating healthcare cost planning into your overall retirement strategy is needed to maintain financial stability. Start by allocating a portion of your retirement savings specifically for healthcare expenses. This dedicated fund can help cover unexpected costs and bridge any gaps in coverage to make sure that medical needs do not compromise your financial security. Additionally, I recommend that you include healthcare expenses in your retirement income planning. To do this, estimate the amount required annually and incorporate it into your withdrawal strategy. This foresight helps balance your budget and manage cash flow to prevent healthcare costs from undermining your financial goals. Addressing healthcare costs proactively safeguards your retirement savings and improves your ability to enjoy a secure and fulfilling retirement (Rower Price, 2024).

Managing Longevity Risk

Longevity risk is an increasingly relevant concern in retirement planning. It reflects the possibility that you might outlive your financial resources. As life expectancy rises, so too does the potential for extended retirement years. This longevity brings with it increased healthcare needs and living expenses that necessitate a solid financial strategy to make sure that your assets last as long as you do. The implications of living longer than expected can strain your savings, particularly if your retirement plan does not account for decades of inflation and the rising cost of healthcare. This risk challenges the assumption that fixed savings are sufficient and highlights the need for strategic planning that adapts to an extended timeline.

To effectively mitigate longevity risk, focus on strategies that improve financial security over time, particularly by increasing passive income streams from a young age. The earlier you begin building income-generating assets, the greater their growth potential.

This allows them to cover your monthly fixed expenses, and possibly more, by the time you reach retirement. Once your passive income surpasses your living expenses, longevity is no longer a concern.

The true value of multiple income streams lies in the fact that your financial base is never zero base again. No matter the amount of income these assets generate, your financial base starts with the income from passive sources, not your paycheck. This means that even if you lose your job or decide to take time off, your passive income continues to provide a financial foundation. Unlike income from a workplace, which stops if you're unable to work, passive income flows consistently, even when you're sleeping, on vacation, or facing health challenges.

Think about it—your financial responsibilities grow over time as you take on more obligations like supporting family members, paying for education, or managing liabilities like mortgages. At the same time, your physical ability to work diminishes with age. Your health and body are limited resources, not unlimited ones. That's why it's important to rethink how you earn money as early as possible and prioritize building passive income streams.

Whether through dividend-paying stocks, rental properties, annuities, or intellectual property, diversifying your income sources reduces reliance on a single paycheck and creates stability. The earlier you start increasing your income-generating assets, the faster and more reliably they will grow and provide financial security that protects you from market volatility and unexpected life events.

Delaying retirement can help mitigate longevity risk as a last resort. Working a few additional years provides more time to earn income, grow your savings, and reduce the number of years your retirement funds need to last. However, this approach should complement, not replace, your efforts to build passive income streams early in life.

Financial products specifically designed to address longevity risk offer additional protection. Longevity annuities are one of these tools. These annuities defer income payments until a specified age, such as 85, to provide guaranteed income for life thereafter. Incorporating a longevity annuity into your retirement plan secures a steady income stream in the later stages of retirement that reduces the risk of depleting your assets. This approach provides peace of mind, knowing that you have a financial safety net in place for your most advanced years. Additionally, longevity annuities can be structured to account for inflation, which preserves your purchasing power over time. This feature is particularly valuable given the long-term horizon they are designed to cover.

Regular financial reviews play a significant role in managing longevity risk because they allow you to adapt your plans to changing circumstances. Periodic reassessment of your financial situation helps keep your retirement strategy aligned with your goals and needs. Adjusting budgets and spending plans as necessary can help maintain financial balance, especially in response to unexpected expenses or market changes. Regularly reviewing your insurance and investment portfolios can also uncover opportunities for optimization, such as reallocating assets to better match your risk tolerance or adjusting coverage to reflect your current health status. This proactive approach ensures that your financial plan develops with you so it can maintain its effectiveness throughout your retirement.

Incorporating these strategies into your retirement plan mitigates the risk of outliving your resources and supports your overall financial resilience. Increasing the number of income streams, diversifying income, utilizing financial products, and conducting regular reviews will help you position yourself to get through the uncertainties of extended longevity with confidence. This comprehensive approach equips you to handle the financial demands of a longer life to make sure that you can enjoy your retirement years without undue worry (Schroeder, 2024). As we conclude this chapter, consider how these insights integrate into your broader financial strategy and prepare you for retirement and beyond.

In Chapter 7, we will shift our focus to the non-financial aspects of retirement and explore how to find purpose and fulfillment beyond work. This exploration shows the holistic nature of retirement planning, where financial security and personal growth intersect to create a meaningful and satisfying retirement experience.

Chapter 7
Non-Financial Aspects of Retirement

Retirement is often viewed as a cessation of work, but I like to embrace it as an opportunity to redefine purpose and enrich life beyond the confines of a career. As you transition from structured work environments into the freedom of retirement, the challenge lies in finding a new sense of purpose. This chapter invites you to explore what truly matters outside professional achievements and to cultivate a fulfilling retirement through introspection and community engagement.

Finding Purpose Beyond Work

As you step away from the demands of a career, self-reflection becomes a beneficial exercise in identifying personal values and goals that may have been overshadowed by professional pursuits. You can begin by engaging in journaling exercises that encourage self-discovery. Reflect on your core values, those guiding principles that lie deeply within you, and consider how they might manifest in a life untethered by work obligations. Through this introspection, you can uncover long-term aspirations that align with your true self and pave the way for a retirement filled with purpose and intentionality.

Setting new personal milestones is another powerful method for maintaining direction and achieving fulfillment in retirement. To do this, establish goals that challenge and excite you, such as volunteering in community projects or pursuing certifications in areas of interest. Volunteering contributes to the greater good and creates a sense of belonging and accomplishment. It provides a platform for sharing skills and wisdom accumulated over years of experience to positively impact those around you. Similarly, pursuing learning goals or certifications can reignite a passion for knowledge and personal growth while also offering a productive outlet for your energy and talents.

Contributing to the community and society supports your well-being and provides a renewed sense of purpose. Engaging in meaningful activities, such as mentoring younger generations or participating in local government or advocacy groups, allows you to leave a lasting impact. Mentoring offers the opportunity to impart valuable insights and experiences to those setting off on their own paths and builds a legacy of knowledge and support. Meanwhile, participating in local government or advocacy groups empowers you to influence change and address issues that relate to your values. These contributions enrich your retirement and create a ripple effect that benefits the broader community.

Transitioning from a career to purpose-driven activities may require strategic planning and gradual adjustments. Consider a phased approach, such as gradually reducing work hours to allocate more time to new pursuits. This transition allows you to maintain a sense of structure while exploring interests that bring joy and fulfillment. Joining networks or clubs aligned with your personal interests can also facilitate this shift because it provides a supportive community of like-minded individuals with shared passions. Whether through book clubs, hobby groups, or volunteer organizations, these connections build camaraderie and inspire continued engagement.

In this phase of life, the pursuit of purpose becomes a deeply personal experience that requires introspection and a willingness to explore new avenues. Identifying what truly matters, setting new goals, and contributing to the community will help you redefine retirement as a period of growth and fulfillment. These elements create a rich collection of experiences that honor your past achievements while embracing the promise of new beginnings (Midyet, 2025).

Interactive Element: Journaling Prompt for Self-Discovery

Take a moment to reflect on the following questions: What values have guided your decisions throughout life? What activities make you feel most alive and fulfilled? Consider writing down your thoughts and aspirations in a journal. This exercise will help guide you toward a retirement that aligns with your deepest values and desires. I encourage you to revisit these reflections periodically. This allows them to inform your choices and inspire a purposeful and engaging retirement (Raypole, 2016).

Maintaining Social Connections

As you move into retirement, maintaining social connections becomes increasingly important for mental and emotional health. These interactions serve as a buffer against loneliness and isolation, which can detract from the quality of life. Regular gatherings with friends and family provide a sense of belonging and community. They offer opportunities to share experiences, create memories, and strengthen bonds. Whether it's a casual coffee meet-up or a family dinner, these moments enrich your life with laughter and understanding. Additionally, participating in group activities, such as book clubs or hobby groups, opens doors to new friendships based on shared interests. These gatherings become spaces where ideas and stories are exchanged to create a supportive network that can be leaned upon in times of need.

Expanding your social network requires a proactive approach, especially as you transition away from the natural interactions afforded by a workplace. Joining community centers or clubs is another way to introduce you to individuals with similar interests and facilitate the formation of new connections. Local events and workshops are excellent venues to meet people from diverse backgrounds, where each person brings unique perspectives and experiences. Engaging in these activities expands your social circle and improves your understanding of the community you live in. Participating actively builds a web of relationships that support personal growth and support life satisfaction.

Intergenerational relationships offer a wealth of benefits and provide insights that span different life stages. Engaging with younger generations through grandparenting activities or storytelling sessions allows you to share your wisdom and life experiences while learning about contemporary issues and perspectives. This knowledge exchange enriches both parties by building a deeper understanding and appreciation for different viewpoints. Volunteering in schools or youth organizations further strengthens these bonds as you contribute positively to developing and educating young minds. These interactions keep you connected to the pulse of modern society and make sure that your legacy of knowledge and values is passed on.

Technology plays a significant role in maintaining and improving relationships by bridging the gap when physical presence is not possible. Video calls with distant relatives offer a face-to-face connection and allow you to share in life's milestones despite geographical barriers. Similarly, social media platforms provide a convenient way to reconnect with old friends or stay updated on the lives of loved ones. These digital tools enable you to maintain an active social life and create connections that are as meaningful as those in person. Embracing technology can help improve your social interactions by making sure that distance does not diminish the strength of your relationships (Kendal on Hudson, 2024).

Exploring New Passions and Hobbies

Retirement presents a golden opportunity to rekindle old interests or discover new passions that invigorate the mind and enliven the spirit. Engaging in activities that spark joy and creativity can significantly impact your sense of fulfillment and mental well-being. You could consider taking up painting or learning to play a musical instrument. These pursuits offer a creative outlet and encourage patience and perseverance, skills that translate well into other areas of life. For those who enjoy more active endeavors, attending cooking classes or joining a dance group can provide both physical exercise and social interaction. These activities engage your senses while challenging both body and mind to create a sense of accomplishment as you master new skills.

Creative expression holds immense benefits for cognitive function and emotional health. Participating in local art shows or crafts fairs allows you to share your creations with others, which builds confidence and community connections. Writing poetry or stories can also be a meditative practice that helps you process thoughts and emotions while contributing to the literary world. These endeavors promote mental agility, as creative tasks stimulate the brain, reduce stress, and improve mood. The act of creation becomes a form of self-care that nurtures your inner life and provides a sense of purpose.

Hobbies need not remain mere pastimes. They can also turn into side projects or even small businesses that offer fulfillment and potential income. Selling handmade crafts online opens avenues for entrepreneurship and connects you with a global market eager for unique, artisanal products. Teaching skills or classes based on personal expertise can also turn a hobby into a rewarding venture. Whether it's offering cooking lessons or guiding others in learning an instrument, sharing your passion can bring joy to others while supporting your financial goals. This development from hobby to side project generates income and cultivates a deeper connection to your interests to make your retirement livelier and more meaningful.

Finding and sustaining interest in new activities requires curiosity and an open mind. I encourage you to experiment with hobby sampler workshops to explore various interests without a long-term commitment. These workshops provide a glimpse into different activities and allow you to gauge your enthusiasm before diving deeper. Setting personal challenges or goals related to hobbies can also maintain motivation and excitement. Whether it's perfecting a recipe, completing a painting, or learning a new dance routine, these goals provide structure and achievement that inspire continued engagement. Approaching hobbies with an adventurous spirit will open you to a world of possibilities that enrich your life (Inspired Living, 2024).

Continuous Learning in Retirement

Retirement is often seen as a time to rest, but it is also a time to invigorate the mind through lifelong learning. Engaging in education can keep your mind active and sharp by enriching your retirement years with new insights and skills. This pursuit of knowledge is not limited to traditional classrooms. Online platforms like Coursera or Master Class offer courses covering a wide range of subjects, from history to science to the arts. These platforms provide the flexibility to learn at your own pace, whether you are exploring a new topic or deepening your understanding of a long-held interest. Meanwhile, attending lectures or seminars at local universities can provide a more structured and interactive educational experience. These settings offer knowledge and opportunities to engage with fellow learners to widen your social connections.

The avenues for continued learning are as diverse as your interests. For those who revel in the written word, joining book clubs can offer a space for literary exploration and discussion. These groups provide an opportunity to engage with different perspectives and interpretations that build a deeper appreciation for literature. Alternatively, participating in language exchange programs can open doors to new cultures and ideas. In addition to exploring a new mode of communication, learning a new language involves understanding different ways of thinking and living. These programs connect you with native speakers to encourage genuine cultural exchange and personal growth. Exploring these diverse learning paths will tailor your educational experience to suit your preferences and learning style.

Acquiring new skills and knowledge during retirement can significantly improve your life. Consider the potential of learning computer programming or digital photography. These skills offer personal satisfaction and can open up new opportunities for engagement and creativity. Programming can empower you to solve problems or develop projects that interest you, while digital photography allows you to capture and share the beauty you see in the world. Both skills encourage a proactive approach to learning and can lead to unexpected opportunities, whether in personal projects or community contributions. Embracing these new challenges will enrich your life with a sense of accomplishment and purpose.

Engaging with educational communities further benefits your learning experience. Joining groups or forums focused on shared learning experiences can provide support and encouragement. Workshops and conferences offer concentrated learning opportunities where you can immerse yourself in specific topics and connect with experts and peers. These events often stimulate new ideas and collaborations that expand your horizons and deepen your understanding. Similarly, online learning communities and discussion groups provide a platform for continuous interaction and exchange of ideas. These digital spaces allow you to connect with a global network of learners so you can share insights and experiences that transcend geographical boundaries. By participating in these communities, you tap into a wealth of knowledge and support that boosts growth and inspiration (Cascio, n.d.).

In exploring the non-financial aspects of retirement, it becomes clear that this phase of life is rich with potential. Continuous learning offers a path to personal growth and fulfillment that complements the other dimensions of retirement discussed in this chapter. As you embrace this new chapter in your life, I encourage you to consider how these elements integrate with your financial strategies and enrich your overall retirement experience. Prepare to dive into Chapter 8, where we will explore the psychological barriers to retirement and how to overcome them for a fulfilling and secure future.

Chapter 8
Overcoming Psychological Barriers

Many people have a quiet worry that often shadows the thought of retirement, and this is the fear of outliving savings. It is a concern that relates deeply with many, regardless of age or financial status, and it persists even among those who have diligently prepared. This fear is not unfounded. Conversations with financial advisors frequently echo this sentiment, as they note how common it is for clients to voice concerns about sustaining their standard of living throughout retirement. Such fears can lead to hesitation in spending savings and drive individuals to live more frugally than necessary. In this chapter, we'll discuss how you can effectively manage this fear and overcome the other common psychological barriers associated with retirement.

Confronting the Fear of Outliving Savings

To address this prevalent anxiety, it is important to adopt strategies that protect financial longevity and peace of mind. One effective approach involves creating a detailed budget that meticulously tracks your anticipated future expenses. This budget provides clarity on your financial needs and helps you allocate resources efficiently. Forecasting potential costs can give you insights into your spending patterns and enable you to make informed decisions about your financial priorities. Alongside budgeting, establishing a reliable income stream through annuities can offer security. Annuities provide a guaranteed income for life, which secures a steady cash flow that can cover necessary expenses without drawing down principal savings. Although annuities may offer lower returns and involve management expenses, they are invaluable for those seeking financial stability in retirement.

Flexibility is another key component of financial security in retirement. Adopting a flexible spending approach allows you to adjust your expenditures in response to changing market conditions. This involves distinguishing between discretionary and necessary spending. Necessary expenses include things like housing, healthcare, and food, which take priority in your budget. On the other hand, discretionary spending encompasses non-essential items like dining out and entertainment, which can be adjusted based on your financial situation. Prioritizing necessary expenses and remaining adaptable with discretionary spending will extend the life of your savings and help you make sure that resources are available when truly needed.

Maintaining an emergency fund will help cover unexpected expenses and provide a financial safety net. Financial experts typically recommend setting aside three to six months' worth of expenses in a liquid account to allow for quick access to funds when necessary. Building and replenishing this fund requires discipline and commitment. Consider setting up a separate savings account dedicated to emergencies and contributing to it regularly, even if only in small amounts. This practice fortifies your financial resilience and offers peace of mind because you know that you have a safeguard against life's uncertainties (The Tennessee Credit Union Blog, 2023).

. . .

Interactive Element: Emergency Fund Building Exercise

To strengthen your financial security, take time to evaluate your current emergency fund status. You can start doing this by calculating your necessary monthly expenses. Then, multiply this figure by three to six to determine your target emergency fund amount. Next, assess your existing savings to identify any shortfall. Create a plan to build or replenish your emergency fund by setting realistic monthly contribution goals. I recommend automating these contributions to secure consistency and reduce the temptation to divert funds elsewhere (Kurt, 2022).

Balancing Present and Future Needs

Balancing present enjoyment with future financial security is a challenge many people face, regardless of age or income level. The psychological concept of delayed gratification plays a significant role here. It is the ability to resist the temptation of immediate pleasure for future benefits. This concept is important in financial planning, as it encourages saving and investing for long-term goals. However, it can be difficult to practice, especially when daily life presents numerous opportunities for immediate gratification. The allure of a new gadget, a luxurious vacation, or dining at a high-end restaurant can often overshadow the distant prospect of a secure retirement. This challenge requires a careful approach that allows you to enjoy life now while still preparing for your future.

A practical strategy for achieving this balance involves setting aside a portion of your budget specifically for "fun money." This allocation is for guilt-free spending on unnecessary items or experiences that bring you joy. Designating a fixed amount for discretionary spending allows you to indulge in life's pleasures without compromising your financial security. This approach satisfies the desire for immediate enjoyment and reinforces financial discipline by making sure that indulgences do not derail long-term objectives. Alongside this, I encourage you to allocate a predetermined percentage of your income to savings and investments. This consistent contribution to your future serves as a foundation for financial stability and allows your wealth to grow over time. Automating these contributions will simplify the process and reduce the temptation to spend that portion of your income elsewhere.

Mindful spending plays a significant role in maintaining this delicate balance. It involves making intentional choices about how you use your resources and aligning expenditures with your long-term goals and values. Before making a purchase, consider whether it will contribute to your lasting happiness or if it is merely a fleeting desire. This reflection encourages thoughtful decision-making and helps you make sure that your spending aligns with your broader aspirations. Practicing gratitude for non-material joys can also shift your focus away from consumerism. By appreciating the simple pleasures in life, such as a walk in nature or time spent with loved ones, you can find fulfillment without the need for constant consumption. This perspective supports contentment and reduces the impulse to seek happiness through material possessions.

Lifestyle flexibility is another key component in balancing present and future needs. It allows you to adapt your living arrangements and habits to align with your financial goals. Downsizing, for instance, can significantly reduce living expenses, which frees up resources for savings and investment. A smaller home requires less maintenance and energy as well. This lowers costs while simplifying life even further.

This approach improves financial security and contributes to a more sustainable lifestyle. Similarly, exploring cost-effective ways to enjoy hobbies and travel can provide fulfillment without excessive spending. I personally like to explore local adventures or budget-friendly hobbies that offer rich experiences without straining my finances. This adaptability allows me to enjoy a vibrant life today while maintaining a clear path toward a secure and prosperous future.

Balancing current desires with future security is a process that requires ongoing attention and flexibility. Incorporating these strategies into your financial plan will create a lifestyle that honors your immediate aspirations and long-term goals. This balance involves making choices that support a fulfilling and secure life. It's important to remember that true financial well-being encompasses both present satisfaction and future preparedness so you can thrive in every stage of life (Raise The Bar Investments, 2023).

Tackling Decision Fatigue

Decision fatigue is a common yet often overlooked psychological state that significantly impacts financial planning. It arises when the brain becomes overwhelmed by the sheer number of decisions required daily. This can lead to poor choices or, worse, inaction. This cognitive overload can manifest in various ways, such as procrastination, impulsive decisions, or the inability to decide at all. Symptoms of decision fatigue are evident when you find yourself hesitating over minor choices or defaulting to the easiest option without adequate consideration because you feel mentally exhausted. In financial planning, this can result in missed opportunities, suboptimal investment choices, or neglecting important financial tasks, which ultimately hinder your long-term financial well-being.

Fortunately, strategies exist to mitigate decision fatigue and streamline your financial decision-making process. Automating your savings and investments is one powerful method. For example, my client Drew struggled with decision fatigue regarding sending money to his investing accounts. He simply felt anxious about deciding on how much money to send each time, not to mention how often. To overcome this, we set up automatic transfers of $500 from his checking account to his investment account each month. This provided him with consistency in reaching his financial goals and eliminated the need to repeatedly decide when and how much to save, which freed up his mental capacity for more significant decisions.

For complex financial choices, decision trees can be incredibly helpful. A decision tree is a visual tool that maps out options, potential outcomes, and their probabilities or values. For instance, if you're deciding whether to purchase or lease a car, you can use a decision tree to weigh the options.

1. **Purchase Option:**

- **Initial Cost:** Higher upfront payment.
- **Long-Term Costs:** Lower overall costs after paying off the loan.
- **Outcome:** Asset ownership, potential resale value.

2. **Lease Option:**

- **Initial Cost:** Lower upfront payment.
- **Long-Term Costs:** Higher due to ongoing lease payments and potential fees.
- **Outcome:** No ownership but flexibility to upgrade vehicles.

. . .

Using the decision tree, you can visually compare the financial trade-offs and practical implications of each option, such as total costs over five years, flexibility, and long-term value. This structured approach simplifies decision-making by breaking down a complex choice into manageable parts, which helps you reach an informed and confident conclusion (Magee, 1964).

Combining automation for recurring tasks with decision trees for major financial choices can reduce the cognitive burden of managing your finances while improving the quality of your decisions.

Establishing routines and habits is another effective way to combat decision fatigue. Creating consistent patterns in your financial activities will minimize the need for constant decision-making, which promotes stability and predictability in your financial life. I recommend setting a fixed day each month for financial reviews. On this day, dedicate time to assess your budget, investments, and financial goals. This routine will become a significant element of your financial management because it will reduce the likelihood of neglecting important tasks. Over time, these habits become second nature and allow you to focus your mental energy on more significant financial decisions and opportunities.

Outsourcing and seeking expert advice can also alleviate the burden of financial decision-making. Engaging with a financial advisor provides access to professional guidance and expertise that helps you make financial decisions with confidence. Advisors can offer personalized strategies tailored to your unique circumstances, which simplifies choices and improves your financial plan. Similarly, utilizing robo-advisors for portfolio management offers a cost-effective way to automate investment decisions. These digital platforms use algorithms to manage your investments based on your risk tolerance and goals. This reduces the need for constant oversight. Leveraging these resources helps to alleviate decision fatigue while keeping your financial affairs on track (Dimovski, 2024).

Interactive Element: Decision-Making Reflection Exercise

To further address decision fatigue in your financial life, I encourage you to reflect on recent financial decisions that left you feeling overwhelmed or unsure. Identify patterns or triggers that contribute to decision fatigue. Consider creating a decision tree for a current financial choice, where you list potential options and evaluate them based on criteria such as risk, return, and alignment with your goals. This exercise can provide clarity and reduce the emotional burden associated with complex financial decisions by promoting a more structured and confident approach to financial management.

Recognizing decision fatigue and its impact is the first step toward reclaiming control over your financial planning. Implementing strategies like automation, establishing routines, and seeking professional guidance can help you reduce the cognitive strain associated with financial decisions. This leads to more consistent and effective financial management. These approaches will improve your ability to make informed choices and empower you to focus on what truly matters in your financial planning, making your path to financial security as smooth and stress-free as possible.

Building Confidence in Your Financial Plan

Having unwavering assurance improves your decision-making abilities and supports a positive outlook on the future, particularly as you approach retirement. Confidence in financial planning is more than a feeling; it is a powerful catalyst that propels proactive financial behaviors. When you trust your financial plan, you are more inclined to engage in activities that secure your financial well-being, like regular investing and diligent saving. This sense of certainty enables you to approach complex financial decisions with clarity and purpose by reducing hesitation and increasing the likelihood of achieving your retirement goals. As you build this confidence, you establish a foundation upon which you can construct a secure and prosperous future.

To cultivate and improve financial confidence, I recommend implementing a series of actionable steps that reinforce your belief in your financial plan. Begin by regularly reviewing and updating your financial plan to reflect changes in your life circumstances, goals, and market conditions. This ongoing evaluation makes sure that your plan remains relevant and aligned with your objectives by providing clarity and direction.

Additionally, I encourage you to celebrate your financial milestones and achievements, no matter how small they may seem. Recognizing these accomplishments boosts morale and reinforces your commitment to your financial plan. Each milestone shows your dedication and resilience and reminds you of the progress you have made. This will help motivate you to continue striving toward your financial aspirations. This cycle of reflection and celebration strengthens your confidence and empowers you to tackle future financial challenges with assurance.

Education and knowledge-building play a significant role in building confidence in financial planning. The more you understand about personal finance, the better equipped you are to make informed and effective decisions. Attending financial workshops and seminars offers opportunities to deepen your understanding of complex financial topics and learn directly from industry experts. These interactive experiences provide practical insights and actionable skills that can be directly applied to your financial plan.

Similarly, reading books and articles on personal finance broadens your knowledge base by exposing you to diverse perspectives and strategies. In addition to personal finance resources, I highly recommend reading books on critical thinking. Critical thinking is an invaluable skill in financial planning as it helps you analyze situations objectively, evaluate the credibility of financial advice, and question assumptions. For instance, critical thinking enables you to assess whether a high-return investment opportunity is realistic or simply too good to be true, which helps you avoid financial scams or poorly considered decisions.

Combining financial literacy with critical thinking will help you develop the ability to successfully maneuver changing finances with clarity and competence. This approach empowers you to align your financial choices with your long-term goals while staying adaptable in the face of new challenges. Prioritizing continuous learning and cultivating critical thinking improves your understanding and reinforces your capacity to make sound, strategic financial decisions that build lasting confidence in your financial future.

Visualization and positive reinforcement are powerful techniques that can further bolster your confidence in your financial plan. Visualization involves creating a mental image of your desired financial outcomes, such as a comfortable retirement or a debt-free lifestyle. Vividly imagining these scenarios reinforces your commitment to achieving them and motivates you to take the necessary steps to make them a reality.

Creating a vision board for your retirement goals can be an effective way to keep these aspirations at the forefront of your mind as well. You can create a vision board by gathering images, quotes, and symbols that represent the lifestyle you envision for yourself in retirement. Then, place the board in a location where you will see it regularly. This visual representation serves as a constant reminder of what you are working toward and inspires you to stay focused and dedicated to your financial plan.

In addition to visualization, practicing affirmations related to financial success can instill a sense of confidence and positivity. Affirmations are positive statements that reinforce your belief in your abilities and potential. By regularly affirming your financial goals, you cultivate a mindset of success and abundance that paves the way for a prosperous future (Anguiano, n.d.).

Embracing regular reviews, celebrating progress, and investing in education will fortify your financial strategy and boost your confidence. With the strategies presented in this chapter, you are well-equipped to face the complexities of financial planning. As we transition to the subsequent chapter, we will explore market volatility and risk management by providing insights to work through the inevitable fluctuations of the financial world.

Chapter 9
Market Volatility and Risk Management

The stock market is constantly shifting and changing, with cycles that can be both predictable and surprising. Understanding market cycles is necessary as you invest, whether you're nearing retirement, in the midst of your career, or just starting on your financial planning. Market cycles comprise phases such as expansion, peak, contraction, and trough. They resemble economic seasons that each bring its own characteristics and challenges.

An expansion phase, marked by economic growth and rising stock prices, eventually reaches a peak, the zenith of market enthusiasm. Following this, a contraction phase ensues, where economic activity slows, and stock prices decline, culminating in a trough, the cycle's lowest point. Historically, these cycles have varied in duration and intensity. Understanding these cycles helps investors anticipate potential shifts and adjust strategies accordingly. In this chapter, you'll learn more about how market cycles work and gain strategies for managing investment risks and mitigating the effects of inflation.

Understanding Market Cycles

Market cycles do not just influence stock prices; they also affect investor psychology. Emotions like fear and greed often dictate market behavior, as investor sentiment can swing dramatically between optimism and pessimism. During a market expansion, greed may drive investors to chase higher returns, which sometimes leads to inflated asset prices and speculative bubbles. Conversely, in a contraction, fear can cause panic selling and significant market downturns. Behavioral finance is a field that examines how psychological factors impact financial decision-making, and it offers insights into these phenomena. Investors frequently exhibit loss aversion, a tendency to fear losses more than they value gains. This can lead to irrational decisions during volatile periods. Recognizing these emotional influences can help you manage your reactions to market changes and promote more disciplined and rational investment decisions.

The concept of market timing—the attempt to predict market movements to buy low and sell high—may seem alluring. However, it is fraught with challenges. Many investors fall into the trap of trying to time the market, hoping to capitalize on short-term fluctuations. But this approach is generally discouraged due to its inherent risks. Statistical data shows that even professional investors often struggle with market timing and achieve success rates no better than chance. The rapid and unpredictable nature of market cycles, coupled with the constant flow of new information, makes timing the market exceedingly difficult (Norton et al., 2023).

A more effective strategy is to adopt a long-term perspective that allows your investments to grow steadily over time without the stress of constant monitoring. However, the concept of a long-term perspective can feel abstract and vague. What does it really mean to think long-term? Is it simply investing money and leaving it untouched for decades? The foundation of a long-term perspective must be rooted in historical data and market performance. For example, consider the history of a specific stock, fund, or index you are investing in. Analyzing performance over various timeframes, such as one year, five years, or ten years, gives you a clearer understanding of its trends.

When examining a short period, like six months or a year, you're likely to see frequent fluctuations, which may appear unstable and cause concern. This is where many investors make snap judgments and decide a stock or fund is either risky or overly promising based on short-term volatility. To gain a true long-term perspective, expand your analysis to the maximum available timeframe, such as 10 or 20 years. Over this period, you can often identify a clear upward trend in assets with strong fundamentals, even if short-term fluctuations exist. For example, if a stock consistently shows growth over a decade, this suggests it has the potential to grow further despite intermittent volatility. Conversely, if the asset still displays extreme fluctuations over a long period, it may be better to explore more stable alternatives.

Recognizing these long-term trends is key to building confidence in your investments. Focusing on the big picture and avoiding the noise of short-term market movements will help you make more objective, informed decisions. Even professional investors cannot reliably time the market, so expecting the same from yourself is unrealistic. Instead, rely on historical data to build belief in the long-term potential of your investments.

Additionally, adopting a long-term perspective does not mean ignoring your investments entirely. It requires continuous study and understanding of market cycles and the characteristics of the assets you're investing in. Knowing when a sector historically performs well, understanding cyclical patterns, and staying updated on economic trends keep your strategy aligned with your financial goals. Combining a data-driven long-term perspective with ongoing education will help you get through market downturns with confidence and resilience (Kenton, 2022).

Maintaining a long-term investment strategy offers numerous benefits, particularly in the face of market volatility. Legendary investor Warren Buffett famously advocates for a buy-and-hold approach, emphasizing patience and discipline. He advises against reacting to short-term market fluctuations and instead focuses on the intrinsic value of investments. Historical data supports this philosophy because it shows that the stock market has generally trended upward over the decades (Bloomenthal, 2022). According to Visual Capitalist's analysis, bull markets, characterized by rising stock prices, have historically lasted longer and yielded higher returns than bear markets, which involve declining prices. This upward trend shows the importance of remaining invested during market downturns, as selling in panic can lead to missed opportunities for recovery and growth (Neufeld, 2023).

Interactive Element: Market Cycle Reflection Exercise

Take a moment to reflect on your investment approach during different market cycles. Consider how emotions have influenced your decisions in the past. Have you reacted impulsively to market volatility, or have you maintained a long-term perspective? Use this exercise to identify areas where you can improve your investment discipline and resilience. Set a goal to review your investment strategy regularly to make sure it stays aligned with your long-term financial objectives and risk tolerance.

Understanding market cycles and their psychological impacts is necessary for successful investing. Recognizing the phases of market cycles and the emotions they evoke will help you make informed decisions that align with your financial goals. Avoiding the pitfalls of market timing and embracing a long-term perspective can improve your investment outcomes and help you achieve financial stability and growth.

Strategies for Mitigating Investment Risks

In addition to portfolio diversification and asset allocation strategies, hedging techniques offer a protective shield for your investment portfolio that acts much like an insurance policy against potential losses. Options and futures contracts are sophisticated tools that allow investors to hedge against price movements in underlying assets. These contracts provide flexibility and risk mitigation in volatile markets by securing the right to buy or sell at a predetermined price. Stop-loss orders are another practical method that automatically sells a security when it reaches a specified price, thus limiting potential losses. Implementing these hedging strategies requires careful consideration and expertise, but they can be invaluable in safeguarding your investments against unforeseen market shifts.

Similarly, maintaining liquidity offers flexibility and peace of mind. Liquid assets, such as cash reserves and money market funds, are easily convertible to cash without significant loss of value. They provide the means to respond swiftly to opportunities or emergencies and make sure that you are not forced to sell long-term investments at an inopportune time. Allocating a portion of your portfolio to these liquid assets gives you access to funds when needed, which supports both your short-term needs and long-term strategies. This approach balances the pursuit of growth with the assurance of financial security and enables you to invest in market fluctuations with confidence.

In the orchestration of an effective investment strategy, each of these elements plays a significant role. Diversification spreads risk across a wide array of assets, asset allocation aligns investments with personal goals, hedging techniques offer protection, and liquidity provides flexibility. Together, they form a cohesive framework for managing investment risks that protects your financial well-being through the ebb and flow of market changes (Segal, 2024).

Inflation and Its Impact on Retirement

Inflation is a steady, often insidious force that erodes the purchasing power of money over time. It is a reality that every saver and investor must contend with, particularly as they plan for retirement. In simple terms, inflation means that a dollar today will not stretch as far in the future. This gradual reduction in the value of money affects everything from groceries to healthcare, which are both key expenses in retirement. Historical inflation rates, which have averaged around 3% annually in the United States, demonstrate the compounding effect on savings. For instance, an item costing $100 today might cost over $180 in 20 years, assuming a consistent inflation rate. This increase shows the necessity of accounting for inflation in your retirement planning, as failure to do so can significantly diminish your standard of living.

To preserve the value of your savings against inflation, implementing strategic investments becomes paramount. One effective tool is Treasury Inflation-

Protected Securities (TIPS). These government bonds are explicitly designed to adjust for inflation by increasing their principal value in line with changes in the Consumer Price Index (CPI). For example, if you purchase $10,000 in TIPS with a fixed interest rate of 1% and inflation rises by 3% in a year, the principal value adjusts to $10,300. The interest payment for that year would then be based on the new principal, which ensures that your investment maintains its purchasing power over time. TIPS are particularly valuable for retirees who rely on their investments to sustain their lifestyle, as they provide predictable, inflation-adjusted returns.

Commodities like gold also play a significant role in hedging against inflation. For instance, during the 2008 financial crisis, the price of gold surged as investors flocked to it as a safe haven amid economic uncertainty (Millman, 2020). While gold does not produce income like dividends or interest, it acts as a store of value that preserves wealth when traditional assets, such as stocks or bonds, are negatively affected by inflation. For example, if inflation erodes the purchasing power of cash savings, the value of gold tends to rise, which helps offset these losses.

To create a balanced inflation-protection strategy, investors might allocate:

- 30% to TIPS for steady, inflation-adjusted income.
- 10% to gold or other commodities to hedge against economic volatility.
- 60% to diversified growth assets like equities, which historically outpace inflation over the long term.

This combination preserves purchasing power and provides a mix of income generation, stability, and growth potential. For example, a retirement portfolio with $100,000 could allocate $30,000 to TIPS, $10,000 to gold, and $60,000 to equities to create a balanced approach that mitigates the impact of inflation while maximizing long-term returns.

Equities, or stocks, also play a significant role in combating inflation. Over the long term, stocks have shown the potential to outpace inflation through capital appreciation and dividend growth. Companies can typically pass increased costs onto consumers to maintain their profitability during inflationary periods. An analysis of historical data reveals that the average annual return of stocks has exceeded inflation rates, which provides a buffer against rising costs. This growth potential makes equities an attractive option for those seeking to preserve and improve the value of their retirement savings. Maintaining a balanced allocation to stocks can leverage your growth to counteract the erosive effects of inflation on your retirement funds.

Inflation impacts your savings and influences how you withdraw funds in retirement. To make sure your retirement income keeps pace with rising costs, it's important to plan for inflation-adjusted withdrawals. You can start doing this by calculating your income needs while considering both necessary and discretionary expenses. Then, adjust these figures for expected inflation to determine a realistic withdrawal strategy. For example, if you estimate that you need $50,000 annually in today's dollars, accounting for a 3% inflation rate over 20 years, your income requirement could be raised to approximately $90,000. Creating a withdrawal strategy that factors in these adjustments helps maintain your purchasing power and financial security throughout retirement.

Incorporating inflation protection into your retirement plan requires a thoughtful approach to both saving and spending. Understanding the nature of inflation and its impact on your financial future allows you to make informed decisions that safeguard your assets. Strategies like investing in TIPS, maintaining an allocation to stocks, and planning for inflation-adjusted withdrawals are necessary to make sure that your retirement savings endure the test of time. As you move forward, consider how these strategies can be tailored to your personal financial goals so you can overcome the challenges of inflation with confidence and foresight (Lodge, 2024).

Creating a Resilient Portfolio

The importance of a resilient investment strategy cannot be overstated, especially in a world characterized by economic uncertainty and market volatility. A well-crafted portfolio is like a sturdy ship, designed to navigate the unpredictable seas of financial markets. To achieve this, it is essential to strike a balance between growth and stability in asset selection. This involves choosing a mix of assets that have the potential for appreciation and provide a safety net during downturns. Growth-oriented investments such as equities offer the possibility of significant returns, yet they must be balanced with more stable assets like bonds, which provide steady income and reduce overall portfolio risk. This balance ensures that your portfolio can withstand market fluctuations, preserving capital while still allowing for growth.

Stress testing a portfolio is a crucial step in evaluating its resilience to extreme market conditions. This process involves using financial modeling tools to simulate various economic scenarios and assess their potential impact on your investments. By simulating scenarios like financial crises, interest rate hikes, or inflation surges, investors can identify vulnerabilities and potential losses. For instance, if a stress test reveals that your portfolio is highly sensitive to interest rate hikes, you might consider reducing exposure to interest rate-sensitive assets. Portfolio stress tests are available through financial advisors, investment platforms like Vanguard, Fidelity, or Morningstar, and portfolio management tools such as Personal Capital or Robo-advisors. These tools help investors adjust allocations, ensuring resilience and alignment with long-term goals.

Rebalancing plays a pivotal role in maintaining portfolio resilience by ensuring your asset allocation stays aligned with your investment goals and risk tolerance. Over time, market movements can cause certain asset classes to outperform or underperform, leading to a portfolio that drifts from its original allocation and increases risk. For example, if your target allocation is 60% stocks and 40% bonds, a bull market might push your stock allocation to 70%, increasing your exposure to market volatility.

Regularly rebalancing involves adjusting your holdings to bring them back to their target weights. In this case, you might sell some stocks and reinvest in bonds to restore the 60/40 balance, thereby managing risk and optimizing returns. Setting specific rebalancing thresholds, such as a 5% deviation from your target allocation, can provide a clear framework for action. For instance, if stocks grow to 65% or more, it triggers rebalancing.

The impact of rebalancing is significant over the long term. For example, during the 2008 financial crisis, a diversified portfolio that included bonds likely saw bonds outperform as stocks declined. By rebalancing and selling bonds to buy stocks at lower prices, investors could have benefited from the stock market recovery in subsequent years, achieving higher long-term returns.

Automated tools like those offered by Robo-advisors (e.g., Betterment or Wealthfront) can simplify this process by rebalancing portfolios automatically. Alternatively, a manual rebalancing strategy—conducted annually or semi-annually—can work for investors who prefer hands-on management. Rebalancing helps maintain the desired risk-return profile and prevents overexposure to one asset class, ensuring your portfolio remains aligned with your financial objectives.

Selecting resilient investments is key to building a portfolio capable of weathering economic storms. Defensive stocks, which are shares in companies that provide essential goods and services, are typically less affected by economic downturns. These companies, such as those in the utilities, healthcare, and consumer staples sectors, often have stable earnings and strong balance sheets, making them attractive options in uncertain times. Additionally, investments in essential services and goods, such as food and energy, tend to perform well during economic slowdowns, as demand for these products remains relatively constant. By focusing on such resilient investments, you can create a portfolio that offers stability and income, even when the broader market faces challenges.

Incorporating these strategies into your investment approach can significantly enhance your portfolio's resilience. By balancing growth and stability, conducting stress tests, regularly rebalancing, and selecting resilient investments, you can build a robust financial foundation that withstands market volatility. This comprehensive approach protects your capital and positions you to capitalize on opportunities when they arise. As you consider these elements, reflect on how they align with your financial goals and risk tolerance, ensuring that your investment strategy remains adaptable and forward-looking.

Building a resilient portfolio requires careful planning and execution, but the rewards are well worth the effort. By focusing on stability, flexibility, and informed decision-making, you can navigate the complexities of the market with confidence.

This chapter has outlined the key components of creating a resilient portfolio. In the next chapter, we'll shift gears to more personal matters by discussing how to create a personalized retirement roadmap.

Chapter 10
Personalized Retirement Roadmaps

Unfortunately, many people approach retirement planning without a clear, comprehensive understanding of their current financial health. The process of assessing your financial situation is extremely important, and it requires precision and clarity. Conducting a thorough financial assessment will give you valuable insight into your readiness for retirement so you can make informed decisions that align with your goals.

A pivotal step in this process is creating a detailed net worth statement. This document serves as a snapshot of your financial position and lists all assets and liabilities to provide a clear picture of your overall wealth. It encompasses everything from real estate holdings and investments to debts and obligations to offer a holistic view of your financial standing. Identifying all sources of income and expenses further refines this picture by highlighting areas of strength and potential vulnerabilities. Here, you'll discover how you can assess your financial health, create a personalized investment strategy, leverage your Social Security benefits, and optimize your estate planning.

Assessing Your Financial Health

Evaluating key financial metrics offers valuable insights into your financial health. The debt-to-income ratio is a measure that indicates how much of your income goes toward servicing debt. A high ratio suggests a need for debt reduction strategies, such as the snowball or avalanche methods, to improve financial flexibility. Another useful metric is the adequacy of your emergency fund. Assessing your savings rate as a percentage of income provides a benchmark for your financial discipline and commitment to future goals. This metric reflects your ability to set aside funds for retirement and other long-term objectives.

Setting realistic financial benchmarks is important for measuring progress toward your retirement goals. Begin by comparing your current financial status with your desired retirement outcomes. This comparison helps establish clear targets that guide your financial decisions and adjustments. For instance, if your goal is to retire with a specific nest egg, determine how much you need to save monthly to achieve this target. Regularly revisiting these benchmarks allows you to track your progress and make necessary corrections. This ongoing evaluation keeps your financial strategies aligned with your changing circumstances, whether it's an increase in income, a change in expenses, or a shift in retirement aspirations.

To facilitate ongoing financial monitoring, you can leverage digital tools and resources designed for this purpose. Financial planning software and budgeting apps offer user-friendly platforms for tracking income, expenses, and savings. Programs like Simplifi and Quicken Classic provide comprehensive overviews of your financial situation and enable you to categorize transactions, monitor spending, and set financial goals. These tools simplify the process of financial management and improve your ability to make data-driven decisions (Yakal, 2024).

Establishing regular financial checkup schedules, such as quarterly or annual reviews, also makes sure that you remain proactive in managing your finances. These check-ups serve as milestones that prompt you to assess your financial health and adjust your strategies as needed. Integrating these practices into your routine will help you maintain a clear and accurate understanding of your financial trajectory so you can better prepare for the complexities and opportunities of retirement (Probasco, 2025).

Interactive Element: Net Worth Statement Exercise

Take time to create your detailed net worth statement. List all assets, including real estate, savings, and investments, alongside liabilities, such as mortgages and loans. Add up your assets and liabilities in separate columns. Then, calculate your net worth by subtracting liabilities from assets. Use this exercise to identify areas for improvement, such as debt reduction or increased savings, and set actionable goals to improve your financial health. This practice clarifies your current situation and empowers you to continue on your path to retirement with confidence and purpose (Ganti, 2024).

Creating a Personalized Investment Strategy

Creating an investment strategy tailored to your personal goals is necessary for aligning your financial actions with your life's aspirations. This alignment helps make sure that your investments are a reflection of your financial objectives and risk tolerance. Establishing both short-term and long-term goals will guide your investment decisions. Short-term goals might encompass saving for a new car or a family vacation, while long-term goals often focus on retirement savings or purchasing a home. Defining these goals clearly will provide direction to your investment efforts and make it easier to choose appropriate investment vehicles that suit your risk profile and financial timeline.

Selecting the right investment vehicles is a significant step in building an effective investment strategy. The selection process should consider your risk tolerance, financial goals, and market conditions. Evaluating stocks, bonds, and mutual funds based on their risk and return potential is fundamental. Stocks, known for higher volatility, may offer substantial long-term growth, which makes them suitable for those with a higher risk tolerance and a longer investment horizon. Bonds are typically more stable, and they can provide consistent income and preserve capital. This is appealing to those nearing retirement or with a lower risk appetite. Mutual funds offer diversification by pooling resources to invest in a variety of assets, spreading risk across different sectors and geographies. For diversification beyond traditional assets, you could also consider alternative investments like real estate or commodities. These assets can hedge against market volatility and provide additional income streams that enrich your portfolio's resilience and growth potential.

Regular portfolio reviews are indispensable for keeping your investment strategy relevant and effective. As market conditions and personal circumstances change, so too should your investment approach. Conducting annual portfolio performance evaluations allows you to assess how well your investments are meeting your objectives. This process involves analyzing asset performance, rebalancing allocations to align with your risk tolerance, and making adjustments to capitalize on new opportunities or mitigate emerging risks. This proactive approach makes sure that your portfolio remains responsive to changes to protect your financial goals (Dow Janes Blog, 2024).

Working with a financial advisor can significantly improve the effectiveness of your investment strategy by providing expertise, guidance, and an objective perspective. Advisors help you do things like plan for retirement, optimize tax strategies, and manage investments during volatile markets. They also help you make sure that your decisions align with your long-term goals. For instance, if you're unsure how to balance risk and return in your portfolio, an advisor can design a strategy tailored to your risk tolerance, time horizon, and financial objectives.

When selecting a financial advisor, consider the key criteria:

- **Credentials:** Look for certifications such as Certified Financial Planner (CFP) or Chartered Financial Analyst (CFA), which indicate specialized training and ethical standards.

- **Experience:** Ask about their track record in handling clients with similar financial goals or life situations. For example, if you're nearing retirement, you'll want someone experienced in managing income-generating investments.
- **Fee Structure:** Understand how they charge, whether it's a flat fee, hourly rate, or percentage of assets under management (AUM). This will help you make sure their services align with your budget (Benson, 2025).

Questions to ask during consultations include:

1. **What is your approach to investment management?** For example, do they favor active management, where they frequently adjust your portfolio, or passive strategies that focus on low-cost index funds?
2. **How do you assess and manage risk?** An advisor might use tools like risk tolerance questionnaires or Monte Carlo simulations to stress-test your portfolio against potential market scenarios.

3. **What strategies do you recommend for achieving my financial goals?** For instance, they may suggest allocating a portion of your portfolio to tax-advantaged accounts like Roth IRAs to maximize long-term savings (Coombes, 2025).

Similarly, if you are saving for your child's college education while planning for retirement, an advisor can help you analyze the trade-offs between funding a 529 plan and maximizing contributions to retirement accounts. This personalized guidance keeps your financial strategies aligned with your goals and instills confidence in your decision-making.

Working with a professional provides strategic insights and professional oversight that helps you stay on track during market fluctuations or major life changes. Whether you're managing a complex portfolio or just starting out, a financial advisor can be a valuable ally in achieving financial security and peace of mind.

Integrating Social Security Benefits

Understanding Social Security is an important element of retirement planning, as it represents a significant portion of income for many retirees. At its core, Social Security is a federal program designed to provide financial assistance to retirees, disabled individuals, and survivors of deceased workers. To qualify for these benefits, individuals must work and pay Social Security taxes for a minimum of 10 years to earn the necessary credits. The application process is straightforward and can be completed online through the Social Security Administration's website. Full retirement age, which varies between 65 and 67 depending on birth year, is a significant factor in determining benefit amounts. The calculation of benefits is based on the 35 highest-earning years of your career, with adjustments for inflation. This formula shows the importance of consistent earnings throughout your working life, as gaps or lower-earning years can significantly impact your benefits.

Strategic planning is beneficial for maximizing Social Security benefits. One effective approach is timing the initiation of benefits. While you can start receiving benefits as early as age 62, doing so results in reduced payments. Conversely, delaying benefits until age 70 increases them by up to 8% annually, which maximizes your monthly income. This decision should be weighed against your financial needs, health, and life expectancy. Couples have additional strategies at their disposal. For instance, a lower-earning spouse can claim spousal benefits equal to up to 50% of the higher-earning spouse's benefit without affecting the latter's entitlement. This strategy can improve the overall financial picture by optimizing each partner's benefits to align with their retirement plans.

Calculating expected Social Security income is an important step in incorporating it into your retirement plan. The Social Security Administration offers online tools that allow you to estimate your future benefits based on your earnings record. These calculators consider various scenarios, such as different retirement ages and earnings levels, to provide a personalized projection of your benefits. Understanding these estimates will help you better plan how Social Security will fit into your broader retirement income strategy. It is also wise to regularly review your Social Security statement to make sure your earnings history is accurately recorded, as any discrepancies could impact your future benefits.

Continued employment can have a significant impact on your Social Security benefits as well. The earnings test is a key consideration for those who choose to work while receiving benefits before reaching full retirement age. If your earnings exceed a specified limit, a portion of your benefits may be withheld. However, these withheld benefits are not lost; they are recalculated and credited back to your account once you reach full retirement age. This potentially increases your future payments. Additionally, working longer can result in higher benefits by replacing lower-earning years in your calculation with more recent, higher-earning ones. This adjustment can lead to substantial increases in your monthly benefits, which shows the value of continued employment for those who are able and willing to work beyond traditional retirement age (Connett, 2024).

Estate Planning: Leaving a Legacy

Estate planning is a significant component of financial management that aims to preserve wealth and ensure that your assets are distributed according to your wishes after your lifetime. At its core, estate planning involves creating a strategy for managing and transferring your wealth efficiently, which minimizes potential conflicts among heirs and optimizes the distribution of your estate. The backbone of any estate plan is the will. This is a legal document that stipulates how your assets should be divided.

A trust, on the other hand, provides more control over asset distribution by potentially bypassing probate, which is the legal process of validating a will. Probate can be lengthy and costly, so understanding its implications is needed for informed estate planning. Establishing a trust allows you to specify conditions for asset distribution, such as age or specific milestones beneficiaries must reach. This provides a structured approach to inheritance.

Minimizing estate taxes is another prevalent aspect of estate planning. Estate taxes can significantly reduce the value of your estate and impact the amount passed on to heirs. One effective strategy to mitigate these taxes is through gifting. This is because transferring assets during your lifetime can reduce the overall size of your estate and potentially lower the tax burden. The annual gift tax exclusion allows you to gift up to a certain amount per recipient each year without incurring gift taxes. Another approach is through charitable donations, which can provide tax benefits while supporting causes important to you. Charitable remainder trusts, for example, allow you to donate assets while retaining income from them during your lifetime.

Selecting the right professionals is extremely beneficial for effective estate planning, as their expertise makes sure that your wishes are carried out efficiently and in compliance with legal and financial requirements. An experienced estate planning attorney can guide you through the complexities of creating wills, trusts, power of attorney documents, and advance healthcare directives. For example, they can help establish a revocable living trust to avoid probate and make sure your assets are distributed quickly to your beneficiaries. They also advise on tax implications, such as minimizing estate taxes through strategic asset allocation or gifting strategies. When choosing an attorney, consider their credentials (e.g., membership in the American Academy of Estate Planning Attorneys), years of experience in estate law, and ability to explain complex legal concepts in simple terms.

Questions to ask an estate attorney might include:

1. **What types of trusts do you specialize in?**

For example, if you want to protect assets for a special needs child, ask about special needs trusts.

2. **How do you address state-specific inheritance laws?** State laws vary significantly and can affect your plan.

3. **How do you help clients minimize estate taxes?**

Make sure their strategies align with your financial situation (Business & Litigation Lawyers, 2023).

A financial planner complements the attorney's work by offering insights into the financial aspects of your estate, such as securing liquidity for taxes or debts through life insurance policies. For example, they may recommend a life insurance trust to provide funds for estate taxes without increasing the taxable value of your estate. Financial planners can also integrate your estate plan with your broader financial strategy, such as making sure that retirement accounts (e.g., 401(k)s, IRAs) have updated beneficiary designations to avoid probate complications.

Together, these professionals form a cohesive team to address different aspects of your estate plan. For example, an attorney may draft a trust to hold a family vacation home, while the financial planner makes sure that the trust is funded with the necessary resources to maintain the property. This collaboration helps all elements of your plan work together seamlessly.

Assembling the right team and evaluating their expertise, communication style, and understanding of your unique needs will give you peace of mind knowing your legacy is secure and aligned with your goals. Whether it's preserving wealth for your children, supporting a charitable cause, or avoiding unnecessary taxes, working with qualified professionals helps you make sure that your wishes are honored.

Regularly updating your estate plan is important to its effectiveness. Changes such as marriage, the birth of a child, or the acquisition of significant assets can alter your estate planning needs. These events should trigger a review of your plan to make sure it still meets your objectives. Additionally, as technology advances, digital assets like online accounts and cryptocurrencies become an increasingly indispensable part of your estate. Including these in your estate plan makes it so they are managed and transferred according to your wishes to prevent potential complications for your heirs (Emmert, 2023).

Proper estate planning will help you create a legacy that reflects your values and vision. Understanding the fundamentals and employing strategies to minimize taxes will help you make sure that your estate serves its intended purpose. With the right professionals and regular updates, your plan remains solid and responsive to life's changes. As you go through this process, remember it's an ongoing commitment to securing your financial future and leaving a meaningful legacy. Next, we'll explore the benefits of continuous learning and adaptation in retirement.

Chapter 11
Continuous Learning and Adaptation

Financial literacy is an important element of financial planning that empowers you to make informed decisions in a world of constant change. Remaining updated on financial trends is wise in today's rapidly changing economic environment. This chapter highlights the importance of continuous education and adaptation, which are important for anyone aspiring to achieve financial stability and growth.

Staying Informed on Financial Trends

Staying informed begins with cultivating a habit of consuming reliable financial news. Reputable outlets like *The Wall Street Journal* and *Bloomberg* provide insights into economic trends and offer a comprehensive view of the forces shaping global markets. Subscribing to finance-focused newsletters or podcasts can supplement this knowledge by delivering timely updates and expert opinions directly to your inbox or device. This consistent engagement with financial media ensures you remain well-versed in current events, enabling you to anticipate changes and adjust your strategies accordingly. Doing this involves creating a daily or weekly routine that keeps you connected to the pulse of the financial world to create a proactive approach to personal finance management.

Understanding economic indicators is a significant part of financial literacy, as these metrics provide insight into the broader economic environment and its impact on your financial decisions. Key indicators such as GDP growth rates, unemployment figures, and inflation data serve as barometers of economic health that guide investors and individuals alike.

- **GDP Growth Rates:** A growing gross domestic product (GDP) signals a thriving economy. For example, during periods of strong GDP growth, such as the tech boom in the late 1990s, industries like technology and retail flourished and presented lucrative investment opportunities. Conversely, a declining GDP, as seen during the 2008 financial crisis, often signals an economic slowdown that prompts caution in investment strategies.

- **Unemployment Figures:** Employment data can reveal trends in job creation or layoffs that influence consumer confidence and spending behaviors. For instance, a decline in unemployment during 2021 in sectors like technology and logistics pointed to strong economic recovery after pandemic-induced downturns. Investors could interpret this as a signal to invest in companies benefiting from increased consumer spending or industrial growth.
- **Inflation Data:** Rising inflation erodes purchasing power and highlights the need for strategies to preserve it. For example, during the high inflation period of 2022, investors turned to Treasury Inflation-Protected Securities (TIPS) and commodities like gold to safeguard their wealth. Recognizing inflation trends allows

you to adapt your portfolio by focusing on assets that perform well in inflationary environments.

Tracking these indicators consistently gives you a nuanced understanding of economic dynamics. For instance, recognizing a combination of low unemployment, rising wages, and increasing inflation might suggest that the Federal Reserve could raise interest rates. This could prompt you to adjust your investments, such as reducing exposure to rate-sensitive sectors like real estate or increasing allocations to sectors that historically perform well in high-interest environments, such as financials.

Seeing the bigger picture through economic indicators equips you to make informed decisions, such as determining the optimal time to invest, withdraw, or rebalance your portfolio. For example, if GDP is growing but inflation remains moderate, it might signal a favorable environment for growth-oriented investments like stocks. Understanding these patterns enables you to anticipate shifts in the economy so you can align your strategies accordingly and stay on track toward achieving your financial goals.

Continuous education extends beyond news consumption and economic analysis. Engaging in courses and seminars builds your knowledge and refines your ability to plan and manage your finances. Online platforms like Coursera offer a plethora of courses covering topics from investment strategies to emerging financial technologies (Coursera, 2025). Participating in workshops can further deepen your understanding by providing practical skills and insights that boost your adaptability. These educational endeavors are investments in yourself that equip you with the tools needed to respond to challenges and seize opportunities. Committing to lifelong learning cultivates a mindset of growth and resilience, which are extremely beneficial traits in an ever-changing financial environment.

To support this continuous education, numerous resources are available that offer accessible and up-to-date information. Financial blogs and forums provide community insights that encourage a collaborative learning environment where you can share experiences and gain diverse perspectives. Engaging with interactive financial webinars allows for real-time learning and enables you to ask questions and receive feedback from experts in the field. These platforms expand your knowledge and build a network of like-minded individuals. This creates a support system that enriches your financial planning experience. Leveraging these resources will help you make sure that your financial literacy remains sharp and relevant (Mohr, 2024).

Interactive Element: Financial Literacy Course Selection

I encourage you to create a list of financial literacy courses that align with your interests and goals. Consider factors such as course content, duration, and credentials offered. Evaluate options from platforms like Coursera or edX and focus on areas where you seek to improve your understanding. This exercise encourages you to take the first step in continuous learning and set a foundation for informed decision-making and financial empowerment.

Adapting Your Plan for Changing Circumstances

Flexibility in financial planning is necessary. Life is inherently unpredictable, and financial strategies must adapt to life's changing developments. Consider how major life events—like marriage, divorce, or the birth of a child—can shift priorities and financial needs. Each of these milestones brings about a recalibration of your financial compass. Marriage might mean combining assets and expenses. This requires a joint strategy that reflects shared goals. Conversely, divorce may necessitate a reevaluation of financial independence and restructuring of assets. The birth of a child introduces new financial responsibilities, from immediate healthcare needs to long-term educational savings plans.

Additionally, shifts in career or income levels can dramatically alter your financial outlook. A promotion or new job might increase disposable income, which allows for expanded investment opportunities. Alternatively, a job loss could necessitate immediate budget adjustments and strategic use of savings. Recognizing these potential changes and preparing to adjust your financial plans accordingly keeps your financial strategies aligned with your life goals.

Reevaluating your financial plan should be a regular practice. Annual reviews provide a structured opportunity to assess financial goals and measure progress. During these reviews, examine whether your current strategies still align with your objectives. Ask yourself: Are your savings on track for future plans? Have your goals shifted due to life changes? Financial planning software can be invaluable in this process because it allows you to simulate different scenarios and assess potential outcomes. Modeling various financial situations—such as a change in income or an unexpected expense—will help you better understand the impact of these changes on your overall strategy. This proactive approach equips you to make informed decisions and makes sure that your financial plan develops in tandem with your circumstances.

Incorporating new financial opportunities into your existing plan can also improve your financial resilience. The financial environment is continually changing, presenting new investment opportunities and financial products. Exploring alternative assets, such as real estate or emerging markets, can diversify your portfolio and mitigate risk. Evaluating the implications of changes in tax laws or policy shifts is also important. These changes can affect your financial strategy by influencing decisions on asset allocation or retirement contributions. Staying informed and adaptable to these changes allows you to capitalize on opportunities that align with your long-term objectives. It involves being open to innovation while staying grounded in your core financial principles.

Setting realistic expectations is a significant part of effective financial planning. It's tempting to set ambitious goals, but maintaining a balanced approach makes aspirations more sustainable. Short-term flexibility must be prioritized alongside long-term objectives. This means understanding that financial plans are not static; they require regular adjustments to remain viable. I would avoid reacting impulsively to temporary market shifts or economic fluctuations. Instead, focus on maintaining a steady course that aligns with your overarching goals. Setting achievable milestones and exercising patience will help you create a financial plan that withstands the test of time. This balance between ambition and pragmatism builds a financial environment where growth is possible and grounded in reality (Siperstein, 2024).

Leveraging Technology for Financial Management

Technology offers unparalleled opportunities to simplify financial management. Digital tools have changed the way we track, budget, and invest. This makes financial tasks more accessible and efficient. Budgeting apps like Mint and You Need a Budget (YNAB) allow you to monitor your spending habits, categorize expenses, and set financial goals with ease. These applications provide a clear picture of your financial health by offering insights into where your money goes each month (Ravenscraft, 2016). Similarly, investment tracking platforms such as Personal Capital provide a comprehensive view of your investments that helps you understand your portfolio's performance and asset allocation (Hoyt, 2021). These tools offer real-time updates and analytics that empower you to make informed investment decisions. Integrating technology into your financial routine will give you greater control over your finances and make it easier to achieve your financial objectives.

Automation plays a significant role in improving financial efficiency. This is because automating repetitive tasks frees you from the minutiae of financial management and allows you to focus on strategic planning. Setting up automatic bill payments helps you make sure you never miss a due date to maintain a good credit score and avoid late fees. Similarly, automatic savings transfers help you build your savings effortlessly by turning saving into a consistent habit rather than an intermittent effort. These platforms can automatically rebalance your portfolio, reinvest dividends, and make sure your investments align with your risk tolerance and financial goals.

As you embrace digital tools, it's beneficial to prioritize cybersecurity to protect your financial information. The convenience of online financial management comes with the responsibility of safeguarding personal data. Implementing strong, unique passwords for each of your accounts is a fundamental step in securing your financial information. Two-factor authentication adds an extra layer of security because it requires a second form of verification beyond just a password. Regularly monitoring accounts for suspicious activity is also important. Staying vigilant allows you to quickly identify and address any unauthorized transactions to minimize potential damage. These practices are necessary in protecting your finances against the ever-present threat of cyber theft and fraud.

When selecting and evaluating financial technology, I recommend considering several criteria to make sure you choose reliable and user-friendly tools. I would begin by reading reviews from other users to gain insights into the tool's effectiveness and any common issues. Comparing features can help you determine which tools best fit your needs, whether you're looking for advanced analytics or simple budgeting capabilities. Testing trial versions of financial apps before committing to subscriptions allows you to experience their functionality first-hand, which helps you make an informed decision. This due diligence makes sure that the tools you pick are effective, intuitive, and easy to integrate into your financial routine. Leveraging technology wisely will improve your financial management capabilities and equip you with the tools needed to manage personal finances with confidence and security (Financial Services Review, 2025).

As we conclude this chapter, you now see how continuous learning and adaptation play a significant role in shaping a strong and adaptable financial plan. In the next chapter, we will explore ethical and sustainable investing and discuss how your financial choices can reflect broader values and contribute to a sustainable future.

Chapter 12
Ethical and Sustainable Investing

Ethical investing is a practice that has captured the attention of investors across all walks of life. At its core, ethical investing integrates environmental, social, and governance (ESG) criteria into financial decisions to make sure that investments contribute positively to society and the environment. ESG factors serve as a lens through which companies are evaluated. They assess their impact on the environment, their social responsibility, and the governance structures they adhere to. These principles guide investors like you in selecting opportunities that align with your moral and ethical values so you can invest in a future you believe in. You'll learn everything you need to know about creating an ethical and sustainable investment portfolio while still making a profit.

Understanding Ethical Investment Choices

The rise of socially responsible investing (SRI) marks a significant shift in investing. This trend reflects a growing awareness that financial decisions extend beyond mere profit and loss to address broader societal challenges. Historically, SRI gained momentum in the 1960s as investors began to question the ethical implications of their portfolios, particularly concerning sectors like tobacco and apartheid-era South Africa.

Today, the drivers of this movement are manifold. Increased global connectivity has amplified awareness of social and environmental issues, while younger generations, particularly millennials, demand transparency and accountability from corporations. This burgeoning interest has propelled SRI from a niche market to a mainstream investment strategy that entices individuals and institutions alike to channel their resources toward impactful endeavors.

Ethical investment strategies offer various approaches to align portfolios with personal values. Negative screening is one such method where investors actively exclude industries deemed unethical, such as tobacco, firearms, and fossil fuels. This approach makes sure that your investments do not inadvertently support sectors that contradict your beliefs. Conversely, positive screening involves seeking out companies that excel in ESG performance by recognizing those that lead in sustainability, social responsibility, and ethical governance. This strategy mitigates risk by avoiding controversial sectors and identifies firms poised for long-term success due to their forward-thinking practices.

Identifying ethical investment opportunities requires diligent research and a keen understanding of available resources. ESG ratings and reports provide valuable insights into a company's performance across environmental, social, and governance dimensions. This serves as a comprehensive evaluation tool for ethical investors. These ratings, often published by independent agencies, offer a transparent view of a company's operations so you can make informed decisions. Additionally, investment platforms specializing in ethical funds simplify the process by curating portfolios that align with ethical standards. Platforms like Interactive Brokers' IMPACT app and AJ Bell provide tools and resources to explore ethical investments (Seymour, 2025). This enables you to align your financial goals with your ethical compass effectively (Benson, 2023).

My Story: The Development of Ethical Investing

Consider the case of my prominent ethical investment fund that has successfully integrated ESG criteria into its portfolio strategy. This fund employs both negative and positive screening techniques to exclude sectors like fossil fuels and embrace companies excelling in renewable energy and corporate governance. Over the years, the fund has consistently outperformed benchmarks by identifying innovative companies that lead in sustainability and ethical practices. This exemplifies how ethical investing can yield competitive financial returns while championing societal progress and illustrates the tangible benefits of aligning investments with core principles.

Ethical investing invites you to redefine what success looks like in your financial planning experience. It challenges the traditional notion of investment by intertwining financial objectives with ethical imperatives. As you work through this environment, you have the opportunity to build wealth and drive change by supporting companies that share your vision for a better world.

Balancing Profit With Social Responsibility

Many investors wonder if ethical investing compromises financial returns. It's a common misconception that choosing to invest with a conscience means sacrificing profit. However, numerous studies challenge this notion by showing that ethical funds often perform comparably to, if not better than, their traditional counterparts. For instance, research highlights that companies with strong ESG practices can lead to superior risk-adjusted returns (Gupta and Chaudhary, 2023).

These organizations are typically more resilient, better managed, and more likely to attract and retain talent. High-performing companies such as Tesla, which focuses on sustainable energy solutions, illustrate the potential for ethical businesses to thrive financially while contributing to positive societal change. This growing body of evidence shows that ethical investing and profitability are not mutually exclusive but can indeed go hand in hand.

Impact investing takes the concept of ethical investing further by actively seeking to generate both financial returns and measurable social or environmental benefits. This dual focus attracts those who wish to see tangible outcomes from their investments, such as advancements in renewable energy or support for social enterprises. Investments in wind and solar power projects exemplify this approach because they contribute to the reduction of carbon emissions while offering competitive returns.

Similarly, social enterprises that address issues like poverty or education with clear impact metrics provide opportunities to invest in a better future. These ventures demonstrate how capital can be a powerful force for good and offer investors the chance to play an active role in addressing global challenges while still achieving their financial objectives.

Shareholder advocacy represents another dimension of ethical investing that empowers investors to influence corporate behavior from within. Engaging in proxy voting enables you to support initiatives that align with your values, such as improved labor practices or reduced environmental impact. Participating in shareholder meetings allows investors to raise ESG concerns directly with company leadership to encourage transparency and accountability. This engagement speaks to the growing recognition of investors as stakeholders who are capable of driving meaningful change. Wielding this influence will align your portfolio with your ethical beliefs and contribute to the broader movement for corporate responsibility that encourages companies to adopt practices that benefit both society and shareholders.

Integrating social responsibility into financial goals involves a thoughtful approach to balancing ethical considerations with the pursuit of profit. One effective strategy is to create a diversified portfolio that includes both ethical and traditional investments. This mix allows you to benefit from the stability and growth potential of established industries while supporting innovative companies that prioritize ESG factors.

Additionally, setting specific impact goals alongside financial targets makes sure that your investment strategy aligns with your broader values. These goals might include achieving a certain percentage of your portfolio in renewable energy or supporting companies with exemplary social practices. Clearly articulating these objectives will create a roadmap that guides your investment decisions and harmonizes financial success with social impact (Dublino, 2024).

Interactive Element: Portfolio Impact Assessment Exercise

Envision your ideal investment portfolio by reflecting your financial and ethical aspirations. Assess your current investments and identify areas where you can incorporate ethical funds or adjust allocations to align with your values. I recommend setting impact goals, such as allocating a portion of your portfolio to companies with high ESG ratings or investing in specific social enterprises. This exercise involves envisioning how your investments so you can drive positive change. Aligning your financial strategy with your values will help you make sure that your investments grow your wealth and contribute to a sustainable and equitable future.

Building a Sustainable Investment Portfolio

Sustainable investing transcends the traditional pursuit of profit by integrating environmental and social considerations into financial decisions. It addresses the pressing global challenges we face today, from climate change to resource depletion. By focusing on companies that promote sustainable practices, investors play a significant role in building a more resilient world. These companies are typically engaged in endeavors that reduce carbon footprints, improve energy efficiency, and support social equity. Such initiatives are beneficial for the planet and position these companies as leaders in innovation and adaptability, which are qualities that are becoming increasingly valuable in the eyes of investors and consumers alike.

The vehicles for investing with a sustainability focus are diverse. This offers tailored options to suit different investment preferences and goals. Green bonds, for instance, are a popular choice for those looking to fund environmental projects. These bonds finance initiatives like renewable energy developments and conservation efforts to provide a tangible impact alongside financial returns. For those seeking a more diversified approach, exchange-traded funds (ETFs) centered around sustainability offer an attractive option. These funds pool investments in companies that meet specific environmental and social criteria to offer broad exposure to the market while ensuring alignment with sustainable values. This diversity in investment vehicles allows you to tailor your portfolio to reflect both your financial objectives and your commitment to sustainability.

Evaluating the sustainability of potential investments requires careful consideration of various factors. One useful tool is the company's sustainability report, which details its environmental and social practices. These reports offer insights into how a company manages its resources, its impact on the environment, and its contributions to social welfare. Assessing these reports can provide a clearer picture of a company's commitment to sustainability.

Additionally, third-party sustainability ratings serve as an independent assessment of a company's ESG performance. These ratings analyze a range of factors, from carbon emissions to labor practices, to offer a comprehensive view of how a company measures up in terms of sustainability. Reviewing these ratings will help you make informed decisions about which companies align with your sustainable investment goals.

The benefits of long-term sustainable investing extend beyond ethical considerations. They also contribute to financial stability and global resilience. By reducing exposure to climate-related risks, sustainable investments safeguard against the potential financial impacts of environmental changes. Companies that prioritize sustainability are often better equipped to overcome regulatory shifts and resource constraints, which makes them more resilient in the face of adversity. Furthermore, these investments support industries poised for growth in a low-carbon economy. This offers the potential for significant returns as the world transitions toward more sustainable practices. This alignment with global trends improves financial returns and positions investors at the forefront of the shift toward a sustainable future.

As you build your investment portfolio, the integration of sustainable practices offers a pathway to achieving financial goals while supporting broader societal and environmental well-being. This approach reflects a commitment to a future where economic success is inextricably linked with the health of our planet and communities. Embracing sustainable investing is a statement about the kind of world you wish to create, one where prosperity and responsibility go hand in hand.

The Future of Retirement Planning in a Changing World

The environment of retirement investing is in constant flux and is shaped by emerging trends that demand a fresh perspective on financial planning. One significant trend is the growing emphasis on sustainability and ethical considerations in investment choices. This shift is driven by a heightened awareness of global issues such as climate change and social inequality, which prompt investors to seek out companies that prioritize ethical governance and sustainable practices. As more individuals integrate these values into their portfolios, the demand for investments that align with personal beliefs continues to rise, which makes it beneficial for you to consider these factors when planning for retirement.

Technological advancements are also revolutionizing financial services by improving access to and management of ethical investments. Robo-advisors, for example, offer ESG-focused portfolios that align with your ethical preferences and provide automated, personalized investment strategies. These digital platforms simplify the investment process because they offer tools that analyze ESG data to make sure that your portfolio reflects your values. Apps like Empower and Snowball Analytics have also emerged that provide real-time insights into the impact of your investments so you can more easily track how your financial decisions contribute to societal and environmental goals (Olson, 2025). This transparency empowers you to make informed choices and make sure that your investments yield financial returns and support causes you care about.

The future of retirement planning will increasingly focus on personalized, values-driven investment choices. As individuals demand more control over their financial futures, tailored investment strategies are becoming the norm. These strategies are designed to align with your individual ethics and goals by offering a level of customization previously unavailable. Digital platforms facilitate this personalization and enable you to build portfolios that reflect your unique priorities and financial objectives. This shift toward individualized planning marks a departure from one-size-fits-all solutions and acknowledges that each investor's path to retirement is distinct and shaped by personal values and aspirations.

Adaptability has become a significant element of effective retirement planning today. The economic and environmental environments are ever-changing and necessitate a flexible approach to investment strategies. Regularly revisiting your investment goals and strategies keeps you responsive to these changes so you can seize new opportunities as they arise. Incorporating new ethical and sustainable investments into your portfolio can improve its resilience and position you to thrive in a rapidly changing market. This adaptability involves proactively shaping your financial future to align with shifting values and trends (Stein, 2024).

Retirement planning today extends beyond traditional boundaries. It involves embracing a future where financial success is measured in the positive impact on our planet and communities.

Afterword

As we reach the conclusion of this book, let us take a moment to reflect on the adventure we have experienced together. The essence of successful retirement planning lies in your ability to start early and stay committed. From the outset, we emphasized the significant impact of time on financial growth. When harnessed effectively, time becomes a formidable ally through the power of compound interest and strategic risk management. Starting early allows you to capitalize on these advantages to ultimately secure a future free from financial worry.

Throughout our discussions, we explored the important transition from being a saver to becoming an investor. Investing in income-generating assets is necessary for building passive income streams, which pave the way to financial independence. Focusing on investments rather than traditional savings enables you to position yourself to enjoy the fruits of financial freedom in retirement. Your money should work as hard for you as you have worked to earn it.

Equally significant is the role of tax optimization. We have discussed strategies designed to minimize tax liabilities and maximize savings. By utilizing tax-deferred accounts and implementing strategic withdrawal plans, you can keep more of your hard-earned money. This approach boosts your retirement savings and helps you prepare to enjoy the lifestyle you envision.

Healthcare and long-term care planning are indispensable components of a comprehensive retirement strategy. We have described the importance of preparing for healthcare costs and mitigating longevity risks. Planning for these expenses will safeguard your financial stability and ensure that your golden years are lived with dignity and peace of mind.

Beyond financial considerations, we have explored the non-financial aspects of retirement that enrich life. Maintaining social connections, discovering new passions, and engaging in lifelong learning contribute significantly to a fulfilling retirement. These elements all benefit your mental and emotional well-being because they create a sense of purpose and belonging as you transition into this new phase of life.

Continuous learning and adaptation remain at the heart of successful retirement planning. The economy is ever-changing, and staying informed is indispensable. Embracing ongoing education and being willing to adapt to new circumstances allows you to seize opportunities and adjust your strategies as needed. This proactive approach keeps your retirement plan solid and relevant over time.

I urge you to take immediate steps toward your retirement goals. Assess your current financial situation, set clear objectives, and use the strategies and tools we've discussed to build a solid foundation for your future. Envision the retirement lifestyle you desire—a life of freedom, exploration, and contentment—and let that vision propel you into action.

If you have found this book helpful, I encourage you to leave a review. This free and quick process will help get this book into the hands of others who wish to financially plan for the future they want. My passion lies in empowering people like you to achieve financial freedom and a fulfilling retirement. Your feedback is invaluable to me, and I invite you to share your thoughts and experiences. I also encourage you to continue learning and exploring retirement planning.

In closing, remember that the path to retirement is a personal one. It is marked by your goals, values, and aspirations. With the right tools and mindset, you can create a future that reflects your dreams. Embrace the experience and take each step with confidence. Your future awaits, filled with possibilities and the promise of a well-planned and rewarding retirement.

I have one quick favor to ask before we part ways. There are so many people—busy, overwhelmed, or unsure—who are trying to figure out how to prepare for the future. Your thoughts about this book, shared on Amazon or Goodreads, might help someone take that first important step toward clarity and peace of mind.

Even a short review or a few honest words can make a real difference.

If you'd like to go further, I also share **bonus chapters, retirement planning tools, and early previews** through my BookFunnel VIP page. It's a small way I like to give back and help you get even more value from your reading journey.

Visit: https://dl.bookfunnel.com/z7tc76rqrj

You're warmly invited to join the list and get early access to everything new.

Thank you again for spending your valuable time with this book. I hope it helps you move forward with confidence, and I'd love to continue the journey with you.

Warmly,

Troy Brexton.

Bibliography

401(K) limit increases to $23,500 for 2025, IRA limit remains $7,000. (2024a, November 1). Internal Revenue Service. https://www.irs.gov/newsroom/401k-limit-increases-to-23500-for-2025-ira-limit-remains-7000

7 steps to build a custom investment strategy. (2024, June 4). Dow Janes Blog. https://www.dowjanes.com/blog/custom-investment-strategy

7 tax benefits of real estate investing. (2024, November 30). The Entrust Group. https://www.theentrustgroup.com/blog/tax-benefits-real-estate-investing

Amount of Roth IRA contributions that you can make for 2024. (n.d.). Internal Revenue Service. Retrieved February 27, 2025, from https://www.irs.gov/retirement-plans/plan-participant-employee/amount-of-roth-ira-contributions-that-you-can-make-for-2024

Anguiano, T. (n.d.). Building financial confidence and investing in yourself. Baker Boyer. Retrieved February 21, 2025, from https://www.bakerboyer.com/resources/articles/building-financial-confidence-and-investing-in-yourself

Beattie, A. (2024, October 11). 5 simple ways to invest in real estate. Investopedia. https://www.investopedia.com/investing/simple-ways-invest-real-estate/

Beers, B. (2024, May 5). Build a bond ladder to boost returns. Investopedia. https://www.investopedia.com/investing/build-bond-ladder-boost-returns/

Bell, S. (n.d.). SMART goals. Mindtools. Retrieved February 21, 2025, from https://www.mindtools.com/a4wo118/smart-goals

Bennett, R. (2024, November 5). Should you pay debts first or save?

Use these guidelines to decide. Bankrate. https://www.bankrate.com/banking/savings/these-guidelines-will-help-you-decide-whether-to-pay-down-debt-or-save/

Benson, A. (2023, March 7). What is ethical investing and how do you do it? NerdWallet. https://www.nerdwallet.com/article/investing/ethical-investing

Benson, A. (2024, August 27). Investment strategies for new investors. NerdWallet. https://www.nerdwallet.com/article/investing/investment-strategies

Benson, A. (2025, February 10). How to choose a financial advisor. NerdWallet. https://www.nerdwallet.com/article/investing/how-to-choose-a-financial-advisor

Best financial planning courses & certificates [2025] | Coursera learn online. (2025). Coursera. https://www.coursera.org/courses?query=financial%20planning

Bloomenthal, A. (2022, December 26). Warren Buffett's investing strategy: An inside look. Investopedia. https://www.investopedia.com/investing/warren-buffetts-investing-style-reviewed/

Boyte-White, C. (2024, September 19). Types of annuities: Which is right for you? Investopedia. https://www.investopedia.com/ask/answers/093015/what-are-main-kinds-annuities.asp

Cascio, D. (n.d.). Life long learning: A path to success in retirement. Dee Cascio. Retrieved February 21, 2025, from https://www.lifeandworktransitions.com/newsletter-archives/life-long-learning-happy-retirement/

Chen, J. (2024, June 7). What are treasury inflation-protected securities (Tips)? Investopedia. https://www.investopedia.com/terms/t/tips.asp

Chen, J. (2023, October 11). What is asset allocation and why is it important? Investopedia. https://www.investopedia.com/terms/a/assetallocation.asp

Confronting the retirement unknown: Facing the fear of outliving your money. (2023, December 22). The Tennessee Credit

Union Blog. https://www.tencu.com/about-us/tencu-chronicles/detail.html?cId=80149&title=managing-the-risk-of-outliving-your-money

Connett, W. (2024, August 15). Social security explained: How it works and types of benefits. Investopedia. https://www.investopedia.com/terms/s/socialsecurity.asp

Coombes, A. (2025, January 31). 10 questions to ask a financial advisor. NerdWallet. https://www.nerdwallet.com/article/investing/10-questions-ask-financial-advisor

DeMatteo, M. (2020, April 23). What's the difference between the "snowball" and the "avalanche" debt repayment methods? CNBC. https://www.cnbc.com/select/debt-snowball-vs-debt-avalanche/

Dimovski, S. (2024, April 1). Council post: 6 tactics to reduce decision fatigue. Forbes. https://www.forbes.com/councils/forbescoachescouncil/2024/04/01/6-tactics-to-reduce-decision-fatigue/

DiLallo, M. (2024, June 20). Biggest stock market crashes in history. The Motley Fool. https://www.fool.com/investing/stock-market/basics/crashes/

Dublino, J. (2024, December 19). How to be socially responsible and make a profit. Business.Com. https://www.business.com/articles/can-you-make-a-profit-and-be-socially-responsible/

Elly, E. (2024, December 16). Tax-free growth: Leveraging Roth Iras for real estate success. Dominion Financial Services. https://dominionfinancialservices.com/leveraging-roth-iras-for-real-estate-success/

Embracing new hobbies in your golden years. (2024, June 27). Inspired Living. https://inspiredliving.care/embracing-new-hobbies-in-your-golden-years/

Emmert, C. (2023, February 13). Estate planning checklist: A 7-step guide. NerdWallet. https://www.nerdwallet.com/article/investing/estate-planning/estate-planning

Envisioning your dream retirement: A guide to planning with purpose. (2024, June 26). Legacy Planning. https://www.legacy-online.com/news-and-resources/envisioning-your-dream-retirement-a-guide-to-planning-with-purpose/

Esajian, P. (2022, August 3). The best income generating assets for your portfolio. FortuneBuilders. https://www.fortunebuilders.com/p/income-generating-assets/

Estrella, R. (2023, October 8). New York Life vs. MassMutual life insurance for 2025 (Compare costs side-by-side). US Insurance Agents. https://www.usinsuranceagents.com/new-york-life-vs-massmutual-life-insurance-which-is-better/

Fernando, J. (2024, February 28). The power of compound interest: Calculations and examples. Investopedia. https://www.investopedia.com/terms/c/compoundinterest.asp

Fontinelle, A. (2024, November 19). What does a financial advisor do? Investopedia. https://www.investopedia.com/articles/personal-finance/050815/what-do-financial-advisers-do.asp

Friedberg, B. (2023, May 10). What are I bonds? Forbes Advisor. https://www.forbes.com/advisor/investing/what-are-i-bonds/

Ganti, A. (2024, June 20). Net worth: What it is and how to calculate it. Investopedia. https://www.investopedia.com/terms/n/networth.asp

Garrido, F. (2024, October 13). Understanding bracket creep: How to avoid tax increases due to inflation. Tododisca. https://www.tododisca.com/en/understanding-bracket-creep-avoid-tax-increases-inflation/

Gratton, P. (2024, October 24). 25 best passive income ideas to make money in 2025. Investopedia. https://www.investopedia.com/terms/p/passiveincome.asp

Gupta, H., & Chaudhary, R. (2023). An analysis of volatility and risk-adjusted returns of ESG indices in developed and emerging economies. Risks, 11(10), 182. https://doi.org/10.3390/risks11100182

Hartstein, A. (2024, February 23). Redraw vs. Offset: How to choose. NerdWallet Australia. https://www.nerdwallet.com/au/home-loans/redraw-vs-offset

Hayes, M. (2023, November 11). What's a tax-deferred retirement account? Experian. https://www.experian.com/blogs/ask-experian/what-is-tax-deferred-retirement-account/

How did the tax cuts and jobs act change personal taxes? (2024, January). Tax Policy Center. https://taxpolicycenter.org/briefing-book/how-did-tax-cuts-and-jobs-act-change-personal-taxes

How to create a financial vision board. (2023, January 18). Discover Modern Money. https://www.discover.com/online-banking/banking-topics/financial-vision-board/

How to stay socially active and engaged in retirement. (2024, December 5). Kendal on Hudson. https://kohud.kendal.org/2024/12/05/how-to-stay-socially-active-and-engaged-in-retirement/

Hoyt, B. (2021, January 6). Personal capital: Free money tracking! Millennial Money Man. https://millennialmoneyman.com/personal-capital-review/

Johannen, K. (2023, June 19). Building your safety net | Guide to emergency funds. FCAA. https://fcaa.org/2023/06/19/building-your-safety-net/

Kagan, J. (2024a, September 16). Health savings account (HSA): How HSAs work, contribution rules. Investopedia. https://www.investopedia.com/terms/h/hsa.asp

Kagan, J. (2024b, October 14). How a home equity loan works, rates, requirements & calculator. Investopedia. https://www.investopedia.com/terms/h/homeequityloan.asp

Kagan, J. (2024c, October 23). 2025 tax brackets and federal income tax rates. Investopedia. https://www.investopedia.com/terms/t/taxbracket.asp

Kenton, W. (2022, June 30). Market cycles: Definition, how they work, and types. Investopedia. https://www.investopedia.com/terms/m/market_cycles.asp

Kurt, D. (2022, February 9). Emergency fund. Investopedia. https://www.investopedia.com/terms/e/emergency_fund.asp

Kurt, D. (2024, April 19). Retirement annuities: Know the pros and cons. Investopedia. https://www.investopedia.com/articles/retirement/121416/retirement-annuities-know-pros-and-cons.asp

Lam, J. (2024, June 25). Savings account pros and cons explored. SoFi. https://www.sofi.com/learn/content/savings-account-pros-and-cons/

Leveraging technology for smarter financial planning. (2025, February 18). Financial Services Review. https://www.financialservicesreview.com/cxoinsight/leveraging-technology-for-smarter-financial-planning-nwid-2023.html

Lockett, E. (2020, April 24). Medicare basics: Understanding what Medicare covers. Healthline. https://www.healthline.com/health/medicare/what-is-medicare

Lodge, M. (2024, May 13). What is inflation and how it impacts your retirement. Forbes. https://www.forbes.com/sites/investor-hub/article/what-is-inflation-and-how-it-impacts-your-retirement/

Magee, J. F. (1964, July 1). Decision trees for decision-making. Harvard Business Review. https://hbr.org/1964/07/decision-trees-for-decision-making

Medina, J. C. (2023, November 6). 6 strategies that can help you avoid year end tax bracket creep. Forbes. https://www.forbes.com/sites/juancarlosmedina/2023/11/06/7-strategies-that-can-help-you-avoid-year-end-tax-bracket-creep/

Midyet, K. (2025, January 28). Rethinking retirement: Finding purpose beyond the paycheck. Coaching Aging Adults. https://www.coachingagingadults.com/rethinking-retirement-finding-purpose-beyond-the-paycheck/

Mikkelson, D. (2006, November 6). Einstein and compound interest. Snopes. https://www.snopes.com//fact-check/compound-interest/

Millman, E. (2020, April 8). Gold price history: Why did gold fall in 2008? Gainsville Coins. https://www.gainesvillecoins.com/blog/gold-price-2008-what-we-can-learn

Mindful money management: Balancing present and future needs. (2023, November 8). Raise The Bar Investments. https://rtbinvestments.org/blogs/news/mindful-money-management-balancing-present-and-future-needs

Mohr, A. (2024, October 15). 6 easy ways to keep up with the stock market. Investopedia. https://www.investopedia.com/financial-edge/1012/6-easy-ways-to-keep-current.aspx

Neufeld, D. (2023, December 21). Visualizing 60 Years of Stock Market Cycles. Visual Capitalist. https://www.visualcapitalist.com/60-years-of-stock-market-cycles/

Norton, L. P., Fleck, A., & Hampton, I. (2023, December 1). Timing the market doesn't work. We did the math. Morningstar, Inc. https://www.morningstar.com/markets/timing-market-doesnt-work-we-did-math

Olson, L. (2024, October 3). The 8 best real estate crowdfunding platforms in 2025. Stock Analysis. https://stockanalysis.com/article/real-estate-crowdfunding-platforms/

Olson, L. (2025, February 21). The 11 best stock portfolio trackers apps, websites, & software(Free & paid). Stock Analysis. https://stockanalysis.com/article/best-stock-portfolio-tracker/

Painter, K. (2021, October 13). Understanding long-term care insurance. AARP. https://www.aarp.org/caregiving/financial-legal/info-2021/understanding-long-term-care-insurance.html

Parker, T. (2023, February 6). Calculating risk and reward. Investopedia. https://www.investopedia.com/articles/stocks/11/calcu lating-risk-reward.asp

Parts of Medicare. (n.d.). Medicare. Retrieved February 21, 2025, from https://www.medicare.gov/basics/get-started-with-medicare/medicare-basics/parts-of-medicare

Pfau, W. (2018, January 16). The trinity study and portfolio success rates (Updated to 2018). Forbes. https://www.forbes.com/sites/wadepfau/2018/01/16/the-trinity-study-and-portfolio-success-rates-updated-to-2018/

Probasco, J. (2025, January 5). How to conduct a financial checkup. Investopedia. https://www.investopedia.com/personal-finance/how-conduct-financial-checkup/

Ravenscraft, E. (2016, March 13). Budgeting software showdown: Mint vs. You Need a Budget. Lifehacker. https://lifehacker.com/budgeting-software-showdown-mint-vs-you-need-a-budget-1764607246

Raypole, C. (2016, September 12). Ready, set, journal! 64 journaling prompts for self-discovery. Psych Central. https://psychcentral.com/blog/ready-set-journal-64-journaling-prompts-for-self-discovery

Retirement savings contributions credit (Saver's Credit). (2024b, August 20). Internal Revenue Service. https://www.irs.gov/retirement-plans/plan-participant-employee/retirement-savings-contributions-credit-savers-credit

Retirement topics—Ira contribution limits. (2024c, August 20). Internal Revenue Service. https://www.irs.gov/retirement-plans/plan-participant-employee/retirement-topics-ira-contribution-limits

Richmond, S. (2023, December 19). Why save for retirement in your 20s? Investopedia. https://www.investopedia.com/articles/personal-finance/040315/why-save-retirement-your-20s.asp

Roth vs. Traditional IRA: Which is better for you? (2024, December 1). Investopedia. https://www.investopedia.com/retirement/roth-vs-traditional-ira-which-is-right-for-you/

Royal, J. (2025, February 17). How to withdraw retirement funds:

Learn 9 smart ways. Bankrate. https://www.bankrate.com/retirement/ways-to-withdraw-retirement-funds/

Schroeder, J. (2024, August 24). How to manage longevity risk in retirement. Kiplinger.Com. https://www.kiplinger.com/retirement/retirement-planning/how-to-manage-longevity-risk-in-retirement

Schwahn, L. (2024, December 19). How to set new money goals. NerdWallet. https://www.nerdwallet.com/article/finance/how-to-set-financial-goals

Schwahn, L. (2025, February 4). How to budget money: A 5-step guide. NerdWallet. https://www.nerdwallet.com/article/finance/how-to-budget

Segal, T. (2023, July 1). What is diversification? Definition as investing strategy. Investopedia. https://www.investopedia.com/terms/d/diversification.asp

Segal, T. (2024, August 28). 5 most common measures for managing your investment risks. Investopedia. https://www.investopedia.com/ask/answers/041415/what-are-some-common-measures-risk-used-risk-management.asp

Seymour, C. (2025, March 6). Interactive brokers vs AJ Bell comparison | updated for 2025. Comparebrokers.Org. https://comparebrokers.org/compare/Interactive_Brokers-vs-AJ_Bell

Shukla, S. (2025, February 7). How to build a resilient investment portfolio in uncertain times? Here are 4 key principles. Mint. https://www.livemint.com/money/personal-finance/how-to-build-a-resilient-investment-portfolio-in-uncertain-times-4-key-principles-warren-buffett-charlie-munge-11738843425403.html

Siperstein, J. (2024, February 2). Adapting your retirement plan: Embracing detours for success. Elliot Rose. https://www.eliotrose.com/insights/post/adapting-your-retirement-plan/

Steber, M. (2024, July 15). Biggest tax breaks for people over 50. Jackson Hewitt. https://www.jacksonhewitt.com/tax-help/tax-tips-topics/personal-finance-savings/tax-breaks-for-people-over-50/

Stein, Z. (2024, October 1). Sustainable portfolio | building & measuring the sustainability. Carbon Collective. https://www.carboncollective.co/sustainable-investing/sustainable-portfolio

T. Rowe Price Personal Investor—Breaking down health care expenses in retirement. (2024, March 22). Rower Price. https://www.troweprice.com/personal-investing/resources/insights/breaking-down-health-care-expenses-in-retirement.html

Tamplin, T. (2023, September 27). Essential strategies to assess and improve your financial health. Forbes. https://www.forbes.com/sites/truetamplin/2023/09/27/financial-health--definition-assessment-strategies--literacy/

The most important questions to ask an estate planning lawyer. (2023, May 30). Business & Litigation Lawyers. https://www.dbllawyers.com/most-important-questions-estate-planning-lawyer/

Walrack, J. (2025, February 4). Types of life insurance plans and how to decide which one is right for you. Investopedia. https://www.investopedia.com/types-of-life-insurance-plans-and-how-to-decide-which-one-is-right-for-you-7482251

Waraker, S. (2023, September 18). Positive and negative gearing: Pros and cons. Loan Market. https://www.loanmarket.com.au/news/what-is-negative-gearing/

Yakal, K. (2024, April 2). Quicken Classic vs. Simplifi: Which finance app should you use? PCMAG. https://www.pcmag.com/comparisons/quicken-classic-vs-simplifi

Made in the USA
Monee, IL
04 November 2026

67383000R00138